ENDORSEMENTS

"In a sad world where the people of God are crawling into bed with political parties
. . . this is a refreshing book. Tim and Shawna have revisited the timely text of 2 Kings
and heard the fresh story of the kingdom of God . . . With elections always around the
corner, I highly recommend this for congregational reading and political reality."

Dan Boone
President, Trevecca Nazarene University

"It's no secret that politics divides not only our country but also our churches. *Kings
and Presidents* is a relevant, timely, and important book. We seem to be confused
about politics on the one hand yet adamant on the other that our particular political
view is right or even distinctively Christian. Tim and Shawna challenge us to think
differently about politics, beginning with the assertion that as followers of King Jesus,
our citizenship is in the kingdom of God. If you are Christian and care (or even wonder)
about politics, this book is for you!"

Ron Benefiel
Center for Pastoral Leadership
Point Loma Nazarene University

"Tim and Shawna have penned a love letter for the churches—and the churches
would be wise to read it! With biblical and theological insight, no less than thoughtful
pastoral wisdom, they demonstrate the possibilities of grace and reconciliation when
we see the kings and kingdoms of this world through new eyes."

Jeffrey W. Barbeau
Associate Professor of Theology, Wheaton College

KINGS

★ & ★

PRESIDENTS

POLITICS AND THE KINGDOM OF GOD

TIMOTHY R. GAINES AND SHAWNA SONGER GAINES

BEACON HILL PRESS
OF KANSAS CITY

Copyright © 2015 by Timothy R. Gaines and Shawna Songer Gaines
Beacon Hill Press of Kansas City
PO Box 419527
Kansas City, MO 64141
www.beaconhillbooks.com

978-0-8341-3531-4

Printed in the
United States of America

Cover Design: Arthur Cherry
Interior Design: Sharon Page

Library of Congress Cataloging-in-Publication Data
Gaines, Timothy R., 1981-
    Kings and presidents : politics and the kingdom of God / Timothy R. Gaines and Shawna Songer Gaines.
        pages cm
    Includes bibliographical references.
    ISBN 978-0-8341-3531-4 (pbk.)
    1. Bible. Kings, 2nd—Criticism, interpretation, etc. 2. Politics in the Bible.
3. Christianity and politics. I. Title.
    BS1335.6.P6G35 2015
    261.7—dc23
                                                                    2015017247

10 9 8 7 6 5 4 3 2 1

For our parents, who have long walked to the rhythms of the kingdom and faithfully taught us its ways:

Gordon Gaines
Marilyn Gaines
Debie Songer
Rob Songer

ACKNOWLEDGMENTS

DIGGING INTO THE STRANGE and intriguing stories of 2 Kings brought a lot of good news and hope to us and, we hope, to our own congregation, Bakersfield First Church of the Nazarene. This book reflects the preaching we did (and the patient endurance our congregation demonstrated) both leading up to and following the 2012 presidential election in the United States. Our church is due our gratitude, not only for their incredible generosity in allowing their pastors the time and space to do things like write books, but also for the many ways they lovingly and graciously engaged us around the topics of the sermons we preached on 2 Kings.

We also wish to thank Hudson Knox, without whose technical skills and punctual dedication on some early Sunday mornings, we would not have recordings of the sermons that serve as this book's source material.

We also owe a deep debt of gratitude to our former pastor and a man who possesses an uncommon ability to communicate the good news contained in biblical Scripture with insight, gentleness, and depth. Steve Rodeheaver first piqued our curiosity in 2 Kings when he opened its strange narratives to us at a gathering of pastors he convened at Point Loma Nazarene University with the purpose of discussing issues related to ministry and contemporary culture. Time and time again, Steve has shown us that, when current events collide with stories of antiquity, the hope of God's salvation can speak through the dross, reorienting our understanding of the situation and allowing an opening for new options to respond. His ministry to us has been a means of a lot of grace, and the depth of our gratitude also drives us to hope that we have done justice to all he has taught us over the years.

CONTENTS

Introduction   11

The Pattern of Two Worlds   27

The Upside-Down History of God's Kingdom   43

Claiming Invisible Political Options   59

Political Engagement and Faithful Living   79

Purchasing Power and the Power to Purchase   99

The Economics of Plenty   117

The Sanctified Vision of the Kingdom   139

Afterword   157

INTRODUCTION

THIS BOOK MAY NOT BE the kind of thing you can discuss in polite company. After all, the topics of religion and politics have ended many a friendly conversation. And this book deals with both—not because we are trying to make enemies or start a fight. Rather, it deals with both because these are notoriously difficult things to talk about, and we'd like to suggest a way forward. That way forward begins with an approach to reading the stories of Scripture that will give us a vision of political life that is helpful to Christians both in the pew and behind the pulpit.

Our purpose in writing this book is to offer a vision of political life that takes discipleship to Jesus Christ seriously and treats it as primary. We write out of the conviction that, when it comes to thinking about Christian faith and politics together, Christians have far too long considered a Christian approach to politics to be concerned with voting a particular way or for a particular set of policies or candidates. Rather than attempt to make a Christian approach to politics about adhering to a particular political platform, we suggest that it has far more to do with entering a different political world altogether. It will mean seeing a different purpose for political life, not simply voting for a different kind of candidate. Part of Christian discipleship has to do with coming to a place where our understanding of the world's systems is challenged, unmasked, and revealed as we follow Jesus. The system of political life is no different.

Following Jesus leaves nothing untouched, unchallenged, or unchanged. But modern Christians have often operated under the political assumption that Christian politics means supporting the party, policy, or candidate that most closely aligns with the version of the church we want to see formed in the world. Rarely do we stop to consider that entry into the kingdom of God may require us to reevaluate how we understand politics from the ground up. Perhaps discipleship to a Nazarene carpenter who was exalted because of his faithfulness in weakness will begin to tinker with some of our ideas of things like power and position. Maybe it will call us to a different vision of politics altogether, and beckon to us to step away from the world of politics we know, toward a different political world.

In many ways, this book is a pastoral letter. It's our love letter to those who long to be faithful but haven't understood how political life and Christian discipleship are related. We write for those who are troubled by the idea that the unity they long for in the church seems to break down every time an election rolls around. We also hope this book will be helpful to those who simply can't understand why someone they know can confess to being a Christian and still vote for the other candidate. It's our offering to those who wonder if the church can move beyond partisan bickering and division, and for those who wonder if their faith might make a difference for politics.

In these chapters, we draw from political theology and biblical scholarship, but we do it in a way that resembles what we've done each week from the pulpit, in the classroom, and at the hospital bedside. Pastors speak into the intersection of lives, where bodies, borders, allegiances, and submission tell the story of who we are and whose we are. For that reason, we've opened the pastoral work we've done in our own congregation to a wider audience, in hopes of sketching the outline of a story that might reorient our understanding of politics—its purpose, its nature, and its outcomes.

As pastors who are charged with caring for and shepherding a people of faith, we have realized that the political landscape of North

America is fraught with challenges both seen and unseen for those who seek to live faithfully as Christians, and our own congregation is not immune. As the 2012 U.S. presidential election drew near, we sensed a great deal of anxiety developing in our congregation. Granted, no one openly campaigned at church; there was no voter registration set up in the foyer. Still, the pending election raised nagging questions about the future, and our people were very concerned with the outcome. Some hoped it would go one way, and some hoped it would go another.

The particular outcome of the election wasn't what tugged at our pastoral hearts, though. Rather, it was what we saw in the way our congregation had been formed to think about politics in a larger sense. We saw that, somewhere along the line, politics had been infused with a sense of ultimacy for many of our people. Whoever won the next election seemed to be what *really* mattered to them. We detected a sense that even those who were deeply committed to their faith were incredibly vulnerable to allowing a party platform or candidate define who they really were. We were perplexed by how quickly people became passionately caught up in the stories of political issues or candidates, and we wondered why that seemed to be so much easier than becoming passionately caught up in the story of God. What is it about politics that seems so much more urgent and real than the grand narrative of God's salvation that we preach every week?

A number of pastoral and theological concerns began to surface as we considered this dynamic. We wondered how our people had been formed to think about political life. We wondered who was telling them the story of what the purpose of politics is and what hope it can provide. We pondered which political world they lived in. And we wondered what all that meant for our people and the unity of the church. Finally, we came to realization that CNN, Fox News, and MSNBC had been telling a far more formative story than we had as pastors. We saw that the people we loved so dearly lived in the political world that cable news created. And that's when we knew we had to begin telling a better story.

Against that background, we opened the book of 2 Kings, and we were deeply challenged by what we found there. We found that 2 Kings invites you into its story, and once you are there, it reveals a lot of surprising truth about the world of politics. We also found incredible hope in the political vision 2 Kings gave us. As pastors, we found it energizing, and as Christians who want to be engaged but are sometimes disillusioned by political partisanship in the church, we found it life-giving. We found a refreshingly subversive, beautifully unsettling story about the way God has worked with God's people across time and the way political rulers and God's faithfulness have been understood by God's people. That story gripped us.

We hope that through this book, you'll be as gripped by the story of Scripture as we have been, particularly the stories in 2 Kings, in which tales of national rulers are set alongside encounters with prophets, priests, and—of course—a holy God. These stories are political, social, spiritual, troubling, desperate, encouraging, tragic, and deeply hopeful.

This is why we have not written a how-to guide for Christian political life with five easy steps for knowing how to vote. If you're opening this book to find "the Christian position" on a particular political issue, you'll need to pick up a different book. Rather, the way to read this book is to accept our invitation to plunge deeply into the story of Scripture, allowing the narrative to transport you into a different political world. We invite you to tour that political world, viewing its wild, subversive differences, and we invite you to be changed by what you've experienced. Stepping into the story and allowing yourself to be gripped by it will be a key to reading this book. Rather than lay out a neatly constructed guidebook to political theology, we've opted to let the narrative of 2 Kings be our guide, and to let the reader consider his or her own political convictions based on what we encounter together in 2 Kings. We will engage a great many different political ideas from issues of justice to party politics to economics, but we will do so as the story points to those concepts. In other words, rather than read this as a textbook, think of it like someone taking you into a story that helps you see the political world differently than you did before you started. After all, that's a large part of what 2 Kings is meant to do.

Part of the way 2 Kings helps change our perspective is by juxtaposing stories with the intent of comparing two contrasting political worlds: the world of kings and the world of the kingdom of God. Following that pattern in 2 Kings, we are going to attempt to highlight the distinctions between these two worlds. We do so under the conviction that only the world of the kingdom ultimately provides the healing and reconciliation our society needs. The world of kings is not always opposed to those ends, but it's often woefully ill-equipped to be able to see those ends. The world of kings tends to get caught up in pursuing lots of other goals, and it tempts us into thinking it can do the task that can only be a result of the kingdom of God.

To be clear, we do not suggest that those in positions of political leadership are automatically and inevitably destined to occupy the world of kings as opposed to the world of the kingdom. Not all kings are bad ones. Though 2 Kings often relishes in exposing the foolishness of kings, we do not attempt to suggest that all political leaders are foolish. Rather, we simply wish to highlight the distinction that 2 Kings makes between the world of kings and the world of the kingdom as a way of providing a political vision to those wondering if the way things work in the world of kings is the only way politics can function.

Our pastoral hope is that the gospel of Christ will become more deeply rooted in our people than a particular political affiliation. Second Kings can provide the resources we need to highlight the distinction between the world of kings and the world of the kingdom, and to see just how different these two worlds are when it comes to providing hope, redemption, and healing. With this in mind, our hope is that, if you are a pastor, you not read this book as a sermon sourcebook so much as a travel guide to an alternate world. Perhaps the rhythms of life in a different political world will be life-giving to someone joining with you in worship this week.

The world of kings would have us believe that a particular ruler, party, policy platform, agenda, or victory can bring about all that we hope and long for as a people. And if we just give them our vote, our trust, our allegiance, they can transform the world. The only thing standing between our present and this promised future is winning the next election. So we must be the winners. If we want to win, we are told, we must crush the opposition. And so we dive into the mêlée, doing our part to assure a win for our camp. This totalizing back-and-forth tells us that this is simply the way it must be and that history will always be written by the powerful.

The world of the kingdom, on the other hand, operates differently because it has seen political life from a different perspective. The *purpose* of political life is different in that world. Rather than overcoming the opposition for the sake of advancing our own agendas, the world of the kingdom understands that political life has much more to do with living faithfully to a faithful God. The world of the kingdom confesses that no political ruler can bring about the good life we all want to achieve. In the world of the kingdom, our trust is placed in the God who has been faithful to redeem creation. And there's incredible hope in that.

Along the way, you may also find that we are going to gently ask you to examine which of these worlds has formed the way you view politics and political life. A large part of this challenge is not to convince you to move to the left or the right politically; it is to ask whether titles like *left* or *right* are native to the world of the kingdom at all. Somewhere in these pages, we hope you'll discover some refreshingly good news about political life, and possibly even come to see politics as a helpful and grace-filled means through which God can give us good things like justice and peace.

As when facing any challenge, courage is required, and no less will be required here. Self-examination is courageous. Congregational examination is courageous. And for many of those who engage this story—or, more accurately, are engaged *by* the story—a graceful fortitude will be required to allow the stories of our faith to look our political assumptions in the eye and speak truth. We stand with such courage and even submission to the work of the Spirit, in hope of becoming what Bernd Wannenwetsch has called "Christian citizens in a torn and divided world."[1]

The first task of this book, then, is to highlight and expose these alternative stories in 2 Kings. Christians are often and easily formed by stories that are not our own. We are often not aware of how influential certain stories can be upon us. Politically, we are formed by the relentless narrative that tells us that politics depends on opposition, division, and fighting. Sadly, that narrative has done much to form the way we imagine the church as well. That story is a worldly one that says achieving a desired end requires opposing and overcoming an adversary. If you've ever heard someone in the church say, "I won that fight" or that they or someone else "got their way," there's a good chance a political story of opposition lurks under the surface. As David Koyzis has written of the church and politics, when we are formed by a story that is not native to the Christian faith, it "leaves the body of Christ unnecessarily fragmented."[2]

We hope that in highlighting the influence of these stories upon our view of political life, we can more readily recover the stories of our faith, allowing the dynamics of a polarizing political climate to take a back seat to the story of God. In short, we suggest that the Christian community not be drawn toward a particular political

---

1. Bernd Wannenwetsch, *Political Worship: Ethics for Christian Citizens* (Oxford: Oxford University Press, 2004), 87.

2. David T. Koyzis, *Political Visions & Illusions: A Survey & Christian Critique of Contemporary Ideologies* (Downers Grove, IL: InterVarsity Press, 2003), 185.

stance given to us by our society but rather be drawn toward a posture of faithfulness that marks an alternative politic of the kingdom. We issue the challenge to ourselves and to the church to gracefully embody a politic that does not move according to the rhythms of power and opposition to make its case.

Our second task is to offer the outline of the narrative that challenges our fragmented stories and reorients our politics. Perhaps, like us, you are tired of politics as usual. Maybe you wonder if faith can or should make a difference in such a polarized political climate. We want to encourage persons of faith both in the pew and behind the pulpit with a fresh and alternative political reality: that of the kingdom of God. We hope our engagement with Scripture will immerse the reader in the rhythms of God's history of salvation, and be so all-encompassing that it sets political discourse inside the larger story of all God is doing to redeem the world. For this reason, we've steered away from making this book overtly propositional. Instead, we invite the reader into the narrative of 2 Kings and allow the reader to take a few steps into the story of Scripture. Granted, 2 Kings is but one room in a large house. But for now, even this one room will give us space enough to stretch our theological legs as we engage the problems, connections, and purposes of placing theology in conversation with politics. At its best, this is what the worship of the church does: It gathers us in on all sides, surrounding us in God's history of salvation and calling us to interpret the world—including politics—through that history.

To put it politely, the church has had an *interesting* political history. That history has often been a challenge to those who seek to engage politics from a faithful position. Most recently, the church has been distanced from political life, separated into one of many neat little modern categories. The separation of church and state, we are told, is that which secures the liberties upon which modern democracy flourishes. Behind this language is a deeper idea, however: The church and the faith upon which it is founded are not political.

But it has not always been this way. From its very founding, the church *has* been political. The Christian faith is inescapably political. Christian Scripture is political. Politics is simply the public life and the life of the public. Faith is public. Attempts to extract the political implications from the Old and New Testaments will pull at the strings that tie together faith in a God who saves and the way we publicly allocate resources, make policy, and determine authority. So long as we associate with other people and go about the task of allocating resources to those people, we are engaging in politics. To be human is to be political. And that means Christians are political, like it or not. As John Howard Yoder has argued so powerfully, the question is not whether Christians are called to be political; the question is to which kind of politics Christians are called.[3] If Yoder is right, we would do ourselves a favor to consider exactly how we are to be political, and to ask in which political world we ought to take up residence.

The early church fell under suspicion by the state because of its refusal to worship the pantheon of Roman state gods, pointing instead to the God of Jesus Christ. Their refusal was a threat to the stability of the society. Ironically, early Christians were charged with *atheism* because of their refusal to worship state-mandated gods. With the unity of the empire at stake, Christians presented a political, rather than a religious, threat. A large part of the problem for the Roman Empire was that the God of the Christian faith could not be relegated to only one aspect of life as many of their gods could. The God worshiped by Christians was the God who had created the heavens and the earth, who lived among us in flesh, died, was raised to new life, and ascended as Lord of all creation. In short, nothing was outside the realm of God's lordship, and this was a problem for the empire. If all of creation was claimed by God, the empire took a

---

3. John Howard Yoder, *The Politics of Jesus: Vicit Agnus Noster* (Grand Rapids: Wm. B. Eerdmans Publishing Co., 1994).

back seat, and empires don't care for that ride. Either Christ was lord, or Caesar was lord. The political stakes were high.

One of the more fascinating aspects of this political collision is that Roman theology maintained a pantheon of gods who served the empire well. They were gods of certain trade associations, craftsman guilds, professions, and the like, making them easily privatized. The god of bricklayers had nothing to do with the god of bakers, to use an example. As a result, Roman gods were easily confined to one household, trade, or area of society. It was not so for the God of Christianity. How can you confine the creator of the heavens and the earth to the fabric merchants or the fishermen? For Christians, God could not be made private. Faith in the God of Jesus Christ was undeniably public.

Christianity was and is a threat to the usual business of public life. Modern society has dealt with this threat much more subtly and more subversively than Rome could have imagined. Rome responded to the public threat of the Christian faith with public recourse: material or physical punishment (loss of membership in a trade guild, public beatings, or martyrdom). The modern era has no gladiator arenas, and we have become far too tolerant to pull or disallow memberships based on religious preference. Instead, moderns have severed a generalized idea of faith from public life altogether. Now, faith is a private matter. Politics, being a matter of public life, seemingly have little or nothing to do with private faith. As Allen Verhey has described the situation, it is as if we modern people hope "to live our lives like *TIME* magazine, keeping 'politics' tidily separated from 'religion.'"[4]

The Christian faith does not allow us to make such neat demarcations, however. Followers of Jesus are claimed whole by God, and this matters for the ways in which we engage the world politically. Any story that would tell us to keep our faith private but that our politics

---

4. Allen Verhey, *Remembering Jesus: Christian Community, Scripture, and the Moral Life* (Grand Rapids: Wm. B. Eerdmans Publishing Co., 2002), 336.

can roam freely between home, work, school, and church is a story that has misunderstood God's salvation. The story of God's salvation is dangerously public business because it claims us as whole people. The scope of God's salvation is infinite, healing, transforming, reconciling, leaving nothing unchanged or out of the reach of grace.

Therefore, politics finds its true meaning and true purpose within what theologians refer to as God's "salvation history." We too quickly assume that political history is told by victorious kings on battlefields and victorious candidates in newspapers. But God's salvation history is often told in the margins. In all honesty, this can be a disorienting perspective from which to consider political life, especially in the modern era, but that's also one of the things we like the most about it. As you turn from page to page in this book, you're going to encounter viewpoints that may cause you to look beyond the divisions and categories modern life has suggested: public vs. private, politics vs. worship, sacred vs. secular, conservative vs. liberal, and so on. When the church takes these divisions as the given and natural categories within which we can conceive of political life, we have already doomed ourselves to think in categories that are foreign to God's salvation history.

Throughout this book we'll refer to this idea in several ways. Sometimes we'll talk about it as the story of God. Other times we'll use the word *narrative* to describe it. Whatever language is ascribed to it, the salvation history of God refers to the faithful actions God has taken and continues to take for the redemption of the world. The ways in which God has been faithful to God's people, and the many events of God's rescue and salvation, come together as a grand story that claims us whole.

It is never easy for Christians to be claimed by God's salvation history when the history of kings has such enticing PR. Those stories we learned in Sunday school classrooms on flannelgraphs feel like a distant memory when we open our preferred news apps every morning. Unless Christians engrain the story of God upon their hearts, minds, and lives, surrendering utterly and completely to God's salvation history, we will go on surrendering our identities to the narratives of cable news personalities. But when God's salvation becomes our history and ongoing story—so much more than a dusty collection of tales from our childhood—our view of the world around us will be transformed as we witness God transforming the world itself.

To put this story into perspective, we must first confess that God is always the main character in this salvation history, beginning to end. The story is not about how a few ragtag misfits are able to escape the logical consequences of their own disobedience and stupidity. The story is of a faithful God who redeems and rescues those ragtag misfits in spite of themselves. These are not heroes we're talking about. They are simply those who are caught up in the salvation history of God.

Second Kings is a curious example of the story of God woven throughout the histories of victors and vanquished alike. The stories of kings are told in conjunction with the work of the prophets and the tales of the poor and the sick. The contrast reveals the larger story being told, that of God's salvation history. Each character is caught up in this larger story, whether they recognize it or not. The same is true today. So we turn to 2 Kings to remind ourselves how God might be working for salvation in the world today.

Because we are dealing with the Bible in relation to politics, we need to clarify some of our own hermeneutical (interpretive) commitments. The way in which Scripture is applied to political life is also complex, so it needs attention. One of the interpretive options available to us would be to say that the political world of the Bible ought to be applied as directly as possible to our contemporary situations and that the role of Christians is to do whatever we can to bring a biblical government to life. This option, however, is problematic in that a "biblical approach to modern politics" draws from various sources that were compiled from several different cultures over a number of years. The political world of Elisha, for example, is very different from the political world of Jesus. While Elisha deals with a divided kingdom that holds a relatively common ethnic and cultural heritage, Jesus's experience of the political world has to do with Roman rule over his Jewish people.

Second, we would need to determine which set of political instructions would be normative in this interpretive approach. For example, the Old Testament seems to give license to making war against one's enemies while Jesus's Sermon on the Mount instructs us to make peace. How are we to interpret each of these seemingly contradictory instructions in a contemporary context? If we attempted a wholesale application of the Bible onto modern politics, we would need to choose one teaching over the other, suggesting that one option is more biblical than the other, which is clearly hazardous for our commitment to the authority and inspiration of Scripture.

Finally, modern political life is far more complex than it was for Elisha, Isaiah, Jesus, or the early church. The numbers of people and resources governments are now tasked to oversee would throw ancient politics into disarray. Agencies dedicated to the safety standards of food and drug production, for example, would simply be inconceivable to a society in which a majority of citizens were directly involved in their own food production. Economics, too, were far less complex. The trading and selling of financial products like mortgage derivatives, hedge funds, and mutual funds did not drive a global economy the way they do today, which is why we look to the Bible in vain for a verse or two that tells us precisely how to handle a global economic downturn. The Bible doesn't give us one single set of instructions in regard to politics that can apply directly, across the board, to modern political life.

Another interpretive option available to us would be to attempt to draw out the "moral of the story" from passages dealing with politics and rulers and apply that moral, rather than the specific contextualized practices, to modern political life. At least two problems arise out of this approach, though. First, if the Bible is nothing but a book of morals, then we are left to pick and choose what suits us, and we have again abandoned our commitment to the authority and inspiration of Scripture. In this approach, we would probably be better off allowing our political imaginations to be formed by other sources, like *The Little Prince* or *Aesop's Fables*. Besides, the Bible rarely lends itself to the simplicity of moral codes. The people we find described in its pages are far from virtuous, and they don't always make the best decisions. Rarely are they archetypes of the political rulers we desire to develop in our world. There is a difference between virtue and morality. Virtue cannot be derived from bedtime stories; rather, it lives in practices that embody something beyond ourselves.

Second, when we look to the Bible as nothing more than a set of moral stories, we will gravitate toward those passages we think support our preconceived commitments and interpret them in such a way as to prop up systems of power that benefit us. Not only can a game of Top that Prooftext be exhausting and fruitless; it also turns the Bible into something that is simply one source among many. Rather than being the witness to God's self-revelation, the Bible becomes yet another book to throw in an opponent's face to attempt to prove just how right we are. Such an approach will only reaffirm the kind of life that is consistent with the world of kings. It can only hope to bend history toward the victors of our choosing. It has no hope to save us from ourselves.

The interpretive approach in this book is one that we think places Scripture in a position of authority without getting caught up in the problems and complexities of the attempt to make twenty-first-century politics operate as a reflection of ancient times. It is an approach that takes the witness of Scripture as *instructive* rather than *instructions*, to borrow Richard Bauckham's helpful distinction.[5] The Bible, we believe, witnesses to God's salvation history in the world

5. Richard Bauckham, *The Bible in Politics: How to Read the Bible Politically* (Louisville: Wm. John Knox Press, 2001), 6.

and to God's self-revelation in the Son and the Holy Spirit. The practices of our lives, private and public, individual and corporate, are shaped by this witness. It is our interpretive desire for our politics to get caught up in the much larger story that unfolds all around us: the story of God redeeming creation.

With regard to the book of 2 Kings, that means we will engage the story of God's salvation as it comes to us through the narratives of a prophet named Elisha. Rather than attempt to make Elisha's politics fit our own, we want to invite you to step into the story with us and, in the process, gain a perspective on the place of politics in the grand story of God's salvation. It isn't that 2 Kings will tell us whom to vote for in a particular election or what position to assume on a particular issue; it's more that, when we step into the story of God's salvation, we gain a perspective on what politics *is* that may be totally different than we've been able to conceive thus far. In this sense, 2 Kings is instructive without being reduced to a set of instructions. It sets the parameters of what kings are when they are in God's story of redemption. It tells us who we are in relation to God and to political rulers. It might even challenge our notion of what politics is and what it is intended to be. And we hope that comes as good news.

Finally, as a concluding note of clarification, we've compiled this book specifically for those who are followers of Jesus Christ and who wonder what that might have to do with the way they engage the world politically. Perhaps you are not a follower of Jesus, and if that's the case, we hope that this book will provide an insight into a people who are called to love justice but who are also called to be unified with one another in ways charted by love, and if we're honest, we hope an encounter with that kind of people might give you reason to consider the source of their hope.

THE PATTERN OF TWO WORLDS

2 KINGS 2:7-15

THERE ARE CERTAIN CONVERSATIONS that stick with you. One of those conversations we had was with Jim. Jim had been a committed member of the church for more than eight decades. One Sunday, just before the service started, Jim walked down the aisle and took his seat. When we asked him how he was doing, he took a moment to consider his answer. He looked around at the people, listened to the music the worship band played, and responded: "You know, I'm ninety-two years old. I've been at this church a long time, and I've been on this earth a long time. These days, when I come to church, I'm not even sure where I am."

Jim's experience at church was one of disorientation. The church Jim loved and served had become nearly unrecognizable. Babies he'd looked upon lovingly in the nursery were now grown and had children and grandchildren of their own. The choir loft had been replaced by a drum cage, and the pastor didn't sit on the platform or wear a suit; sometimes she even wore jeans! The people in the pews talked about things that were unfamiliar. The church Jim knew had faded into the recesses of his memory. As familiar forms and styles of worship were replaced with newer expressions, there was a sense, by those who had been oriented with the old, of being displaced. Jim had always been a beloved part of our community, but it was harder and harder for him to see precisely where he fit in to this place and people he called his church.

STEPPING INTO THE STORY

Jim is not the only one to ever feel displaced and disoriented by the world, and even the church around him. The book of 2 Kings opens in a setting of great and terrible disorientation. The people of Israel have been in the Promised Land God gave to them for generations. They have built homes, raised children, planted fields, buried loved ones, worshiped in the temple.

And then come the Babylonians. When the Babylonians come, they bring utter desolation to the northern kingdom of Israel. The Israelites have seen war and destruction before. What is so uniquely awful about the Babylonian style of war-making, though, is that they carry away many of the people of Israel from the Promised Land. The place God covenanted with their ancestors to give them—the hills and valleys where the people of Israel have dreamed of living and dying—is taken from them, and the uprooted Israelites are replanted far away in Babylon. As this Babylonian displacement is occurring, they are told they can still go about some of their practices. They can still have their priests and read scriptures about their God. Essentially, they are told to go about life as usual. The problem is that nothing is usual anymore.

In the midst of this disorientation and discomfort of displacement, God lays it on the heart of one Israelite scholar to write a history of the people of God. This history will give them their bearings in the midst of deep disorientation. This history will remind them who they are—but more importantly, whose they are—in a land where nothing is familiar and nothing belongs to them.

If we read 1 and 2 Kings carefully, we see that these books aren't like normal history books. Most histories tell the stories of who was in power at a particular time and what that ruler did with the power. In a normal history, you spend a lot of time talking about the coronation of kings. Most histories develop around who won wars or who got rich or who gained land while footnoting at whose expense these gains were made. History, we have learned, is written by the victors. But this author of 2 Kings gives an awful lot of attention to losers. There are a lot of powerless people who seem to show up in this history. It's as if this author is writing about a different kind of kingdom altogether, almost as though this history describes a parallel universe.

In the opening chapter of 2 Kings, the writer spills a lot of ink to tell a story that would be downright peculiar in most history books. This author doesn't seem to want to recount stories about kings doing celebrated things or achieving distinguished accomplishments in the way other history books are written. Rather than recounting the king's glorious victories on the battlefield or testifying to his wise and prosperous reign, the first chapter of this history is filled with the folly of kings doing things like dying, falling through lattices, and throwing themselves at the mercy of a strange, hairy old man.

Then, chapter 2 takes great care to detail the passing of a garment of clothing from one prophet to another. It doesn't take us long to deduce where the real power lies here. It is not with the befuddled kings, though they sit on thrones and lead armies. Rather, this history demonstrates that the real power is that of God working in and through the humble, faithful servants of the Lord. Apparently, it is more important for the identity of the people of Israel that they remember the transition of these prophets than hear the tales of coronations and battle victories. And even in the midst of great disorientation, this history carefully orients us around what matters: the Spirit of God leading the people of God through the work of faithful servants.

Even though he doesn't wear a crown, Elijah is a household name in Israel. His showdown with Jezebel and the prophets of Ba'al have made him somewhat of a hero to the devoted worshipers of Yahweh. That episode established him in Israel's memory as a paragon of faithfulness at a time when faithfulness seemed to be in short supply among Israel's leadership. At the same time of Elijah's ministry, Israel experiences a spate of questionable political leadership. The kings in those days are many things, but faithful they are not. And so, though Israel may have bumbling idolaters for kings, at least they have Elijah. Elijah serves God faithfully during the reign of wicked and faithless kings. He speaks for God when the kings are faithless. When Elijah speaks, it is as if his words pierce the clouds of unfaithfulness that have descended around Israel in the reign of faithless kings. The power and Spirit of God clearly rest upon this prophet who is really leading Israel in ways the kings could not begin to understand, and Israel comes to trust that in a deep way.

Everyone knows Elijah. But no one knows Elisha. Elisha is the son of a farmer, and a very young man who has not yet spoken for God. Imagine, then, what it might be like to learn that the prophet of Israel—the one who speaks for God when kings turn away from righteousness, the one who feeds the poor when famine starves them, the one who defends the weak when foreign armies oppress them, the one upon whom the Spirit of God rests—has been taken from them. Imagine the feelings of disorientation and chaos that accompany losing the one constant, faithful person who spoke for God and unified the people in the midst of chaos and change.

Elisha is not ready to let go of Elijah either. But he senses that change is coming, so he takes up the position of Elijah's shadow, relentlessly following Elijah wherever he goes. Even when Elisha is told to stay behind, he follows anyway. Finally, Elijah turns to this shadow and asks him what he wants. Elisha's answer is bold: "A double portion of your spirit" (2 Kings 2:9). At first, the answer is shocking. What arrogance is afforded to youth! It sounds as if Elisha is saying,

"I want to be twice the prophet you are." But in historical context, Elisha is making the same request an eldest son would ask of his father. In ancient Israel, fathers divide up their possessions among their sons. Whatever the father has earned throughout his life goes to his sons. But the eldest son, the primary heir of the family, receives a double portion of whatever the other sons receive. And so when the young, unknown Elisha comes to the great prophet Elijah with this request, we might interpret his response in these words: "Could I be a son to you? I do not share your DNA, but if you're willing, could I call you my father? Would you make me your heir and allow me to inherit the legacy you have built? Not your money or your land, but your spirit, the power of your faithfulness to a holy God."

Shortly after Elisha makes his request, Elijah is taken up into heaven in a scene that would put even the most opulent Las Vegas show to shame. Whisked away in a vision of wind and fire, Elijah disappears from sight, and—like a son grieving a father who has died—Elisha is left standing alone in the dark. Almost by instinct, Elisha cries out, "My father! My father" (2 Kings 2:12). Then, walking over to where Elijah's cloak fell on the ground, he picks up the only tangible reminder of the man he hoped would call him son, and silently drapes himself in the great prophet's garment.

There are certain people who can be easily identified with clothing that sets them apart from others. Mark Zuckerberg, the billionaire founder of Facebook, is often pegged as one of the most poorly dressed people in the world. Rather than "looking like a million bucks"—which Zuckerburg has, many times over—a drab, gray, hooded sweatshirt over a drab, gray t-shirt has become a ubiquitous and recognizable staple of his wardrobe, even when he is courting donors or sitting in important business meetings. It's not even that he just happens to have one favorite shirt that he wears often. In a recent Q&A, he was asked about his familiar attire. His response? He doesn't have just one shirt he wears all the time. He actually has a closet full of the same kind of shirt.[6] He goes on in the article to explain why he dresses so modestly when he could afford Armani, but the point is, people see the sweatshirt and know that is Mark Zuckerberg. Without it, he's just another guy on the street.

In many ways, this familiarity is what takes place as Elijah passes his cloak on to Elisha. In the days of Elisha, many people only had one cloak. They may have had many sets of inner clothing, but the outer garment—the cloak—was what made someone recognizable from a distance. Some translations of 2 Kings refer to this garment as a mantle, which is where we get the phrase "passing the mantle." The mantle was a highly functional piece of clothing. It was a shield from the windswept sand, a barricade against the sun's powerful heat, and at night, when the temperatures dropped, it could keep people warm. The cloak was far more than a fashion accessory; it was a necessity.

When we hear Jesus teach his disciples that they should give up their cloak when asked for a shirt, we begin to see the magnitude of that teaching. Mantles were one of those things necessary for survival. It also said a lot about who you were. If you were rich, you probably had an ornate and decorated mantle while the poor had plain mantles. The point, of course, is that your mantle said a lot about who you were, and where you came from, and it eventually became a highly recognizable part of the way people knew you. When someone was a long way off, before you could make out their facial features, you could recognize their mantle and know who they were.

With this in mind, let's imagine the scene of the company of prophets who are gathered at the banks of the Jordan that day. They've seen Elijah, their prophet of the most high God, and the young, unknown Elisha walk to the bank of the river. They've seen Elijah take off his cloak and tap the waters of the river. They've seen the waters

6. http://www.telegraph.co.uk/technology/facebook/11217273/Facebooks-Mark-Zuckerberg-Why-I-wear-the-same-T-shirt-every-day.html. Accessed January 2, 2015.

of the river recede, opening a pathway of dry ground for both Elijah and Elisha to walk across, and they've seen the two men walk away from them until they can't be seen any more. They wait and they wait and they wait—until they see the water of the river begin to recede once again. They see a pathway of dry ground appear, and a man walking toward them across the newly created corridor. They squint to try to see the man's face, but his mantle is far more recognizable. It is the mantle of Elijah, the prophet of the most high God. And as the man draws near and they begin to make out the features of his face, they realize this isn't the great prophet but the young unknown who now bears the mantle of Elijah. It probably doesn't take them long to understand what this means: The same spirit that has been Elijah's now rests on Elisha. A better way to say it, perhaps, is that there is a continuity to God's faithfulness that doesn't stop from one generation to the next.

Now, it's good to be honest about how amazing the story of Elijah being taken into heaven is. And it's well and good to stand in awe at the spectacle of wind and fire. But we also want to be sure that the meaning of what's taking place here isn't swept up in the spectacle. While it's true that this story contains elements of Elijah being honored for his faithfulness, and while it's true that there are hints of God's power to reclaim a prophet, the message we don't want to lose is the story of God's unyielding faithfulness to speak from one generation to another. It is the story of the continuity of a God who does not leave or abandon God's people in a time of change.

Remember, when this story is first written down, the people of Israel are being ruled over by foreign kings in a foreign land. Children are born who have never set foot in the Promised Land, never worshiped in the temple. This story is indeed more important than the coronation of kings because this story reminds them that—even without Elijah, without the Promised Land or the temple, even with all they have lost—the faithfulness of God remains. Just as the mantle of Elijah is not lost but passed to Elisha, so the Spirit of God continues to be upon them; God's voice will still speak.

STEPPING INTO THE KINGDOM

In the same way this story is the word of God for the people of Israel living in exile, this story becomes the word of God for us today. Our context has changed, but change is a constant. In the face of constant change, this story becomes a fantastic reminder of God's faithfulness in the midst of political changes, and is a good jumping-off point to begin to understand the way 2 Kings illuminates how the world of the kingdom understands political life differently than the world of kings.

Politically, we see this changing of the guard each election cycle. You may have noticed how divided the United States becomes in regard to a leadership change. Up until the election night of 2012, statistical averages showed that about half the country wanted to see a change in leadership and the other half were happy with the current leadership, or at least preferred it to the alternative. Our congregation reflected the statistical averages for evangelicals. However, those statistics are changing. Evangelicals are not nearly as homogeneous as they were in the 1990s. Especially among young evangelicals, there is greater and greater political diversity. Within our congregation there were faithful followers of Jesus Christ on both sides of the political aisle. Some hoped for change. Some longed for continuity. But together, both groups made up the body of Christ. More than that, God was going to be faithful in the midst of continuity or change; the church would continue to be the church, and the people would continue to be faithful. For this, we gave thanks to God.

Just before the election, the circus came to our town. An actual circus would probably have been more entertaining and lively, but the arriving spectacle was *Air Force One* landing at our local airport so that President Obama could dedicate a nearby monument to Cesar Chavez. We happened to be in that part of town that morning and decided to drive over to witness the big event. We spotted a wonderful woman from our congregation who had seen every presidential visit to town since the Nixon administration, and we took our place on the sidewalk beside her.

As we waited for the plane to arrive, we also witnessed a lot of broken humanity. People carrying signs lined both sides of the street and both sides of the political spectrum, all determined to be seen by the president, and for the clever slogans scrawled across their signs to impact his decision-making. At one point, a lively conversation between two men nearby almost came to blows. These grown men had a disagreement about which candidate should occupy office after the election, but their discourse was fractured. As we backed away from potential physical harm, we watched as the conversation escalated in volume and vehemence. Then, after the plane landed, the president boarded a car, and his motorcade went speeding out of the airport—in the opposite direction of the sign holders. The two men looked at each other, seeming to realizing their respective messages would never be received by the other—or by the president—and they sheepishly turned away, signs in hand, and silently parted company.

In the face of an impending political change, these two men demonstrated just how beholden they had become to the world of kings. Here's a part of what we saw: These men were desperate in the face of change. They each needed the change to go their way. They both probably had good reasons for their positions, but the larger story was that they were desperate for change to go their way because all they had to hold onto in this time of change was the possibility that their guy would win. There wasn't a hope beyond the winner of that election, and it showed in the way these men nearly began to bludgeon each other. That kind of desperation fractures relationships, setting people against one another, and that dynamic is simply the way life works in the world of kings. In that world, if you are going to have hope in the face of change, your hope lies only in your guy ascending to the throne. Your hope will lie solely in the fact that you be on the winner's side.

Consider what 2 Kings might be telling us about this kind of political vision, though. At the outset of Elisha's ministry, a disruptive change of leadership, a destabilizing and disorienting shift, are overshadowed by a larger theological reality: The same God who spoke through Elijah is still going to speak through Elisha. The goodness in Elijah's leadership wasn't actually found in Elijah at all; it was in the way Elijah cloaked himself in God's faithfulness. And now, Elisha wears that same cloak.

Right away, 2 Kings seems to suggest that the continuity of good leadership has a lot more to do with God's faithfulness than it does with winners and losers. It seems to remind us that the story of God doesn't need to advance upon the backs of victors. Instead, it advances upon the backs of those who are willing to cloak themselves in faithfulness to God.

In fact, even in the story of Elijah and Elisha, it is the mantle—the representation of God's anointing—that remains, even when the man wearing it disappears. The passing of the mantle doesn't mean that Elisha won the election for head prophet, beating out Elijah for the chance to wear the cloak. Rather, Elisha's donning of the mantle means that he is covered in God's grace. And when he comes back through the waters, it is the mantle and not the man that the other prophets recognize and respect.

We want to be careful here not to compare the propetic mantle to a political office. We've heard many people say, throughout different presidencies, "I respect the office even if I don't respect the person." The mantle in this story is not a political exploit or national icon. It is a prophetic symbol of God's presence, an icon of the world of the kingdom. In fact, this mantle is being passed while kings are being deposed. The presence of God rules over and above political offices. And while kings and kingdoms come and go, God's faithfulness remains.

But the differences between the mantle and the political office are precisely the point. They *are* different from one another. They operate according to a different rhythm of life, a different kind of logic, and that is what we are supposed to see. If you were to read through 2 Kings 1, the whole chapter is consumed with the transition and succession of kings. What will happen if the king is injured? What will happen if the king dies? Who will take the king's place? What will happen in the interim? Who will be the winner in the transition? Who will be the loser? What will that mean for the people? As we encounter chapter 2, however, the message becomes clear: The mantle of the prophet is incredibly different from the crown of the king. The mantle of the prophet says to us that the same God who spoke through one prophet will speak through the next. In other words, in the world of the kingdom, we don't need to fear times of disorientation and transition as those in the world of kings do. No matter who picks up the mantle and puts it on, it will be the same God speaking through that person. And if that is truly the case, leadership isn't about winners and losers because whoever is in the position to speak will be telling the same story as the person before.

We need to be able to recognize these differences between the world of kings and the world of the kingdom. And as we begin to notice them, we need to ask in which world we most readily live. We need to ask which world we truly believe will make a difference. We need to ask which world can actually deliver hope beyond the anxiety of the election cycle and the fear of regime change. We need to ask ourselves how each way of viewing political life can bring about things like justice and reconciliation.

We should also remember that 2 Kings was compiled in a time of incredible political disorientation. Those who hear and tell the stories of Elisha are the same ones who wrestle with what is coming next, or what the next change in political leadership will mean for them. And that can create a fair amount of anxiety. When Elisha emerges from the Jordan River, then, cloaked in the same mantle that Elijah wore, it sends a signal to those who are reading between the lines in the midst of political disorientation: *Remember which world you live in.* Remember that the world of kings will always be based on who has won, and how the winner writes the story. But also remember that in the world of the kingdom of God, God's faithfulness is passed from one leader to the next. Remember that leaders are not determined by who wins but by on whom the Spirit of God rests. And if you're going to live in the world of the kingdom, follow those leaders. There will be hope there.

Of course, this is not a dismissal of political leaders. It is right and good to desire that our political leaders have the virtues that God calls forth to transform the world. We should long to see leaders who defend the poor, the widow, the orphan. We should crave political leaders who are selfless and compassionate, outraged by injustice and steady in crisis. But the ability of these leaders to enact any kind of true transformation depends on the hand and blessing of God, not the other way around.

Because we desire the transformation of the world, we reject a kind of escapism where politics don't make any difference to us. We don't suggest that we can simply stand by and watch the world crumble around us, because that is not consistent with people who are called to abide in God's kingdom. In 2 Kings, and lots of other places in Scripture, God uses political rulers for God's purposes, so we aren't saying that political rulers are unimportant. Rather, the faithfulness of God is that which captures our hope and imagination far more than the outcome of the latest election. Second Kings opens a tale of two worlds for us. In one world, the story is written according to who wins and who loses. In the other world, the story is written according to God's faithfulness. And we are hopeful that encountering these two worlds, seeing the patterns of life in each and the ways they work, will cause us to rejoice when justice is enacted wherever we see it. We simply need to be aware that the worlds operate differently from one another, and that we may not be able to expect things like the establishment of God's kingdom from a world that works according to a different logic.

For this reason, as the election drew near in 2012, we encouraged our people to participate, to become educated about the local and national propositions and candidates, to engage the political process. But we also talked with them about what it might mean to be handed one of those "I Voted" stickers, and to be sure that, when we affix that sticker to our chest, it doesn't hide the cross. After all, the cross has bought us our inheritance.

As a brief aside, let's talk for a moment about this dynamic as it is unfolding in the church. As statisticians are busy drawing political lines along state borders, race, and gender, the category of age has become increasingly important. Youth will always have a different view of the world they have newly engaged. But especially recently, young people vote based on a different value system than their parents and grandparents. This change is true of young evangelicals as well. A party's stance on abortion and gay marriage are not the only religious issues young voters see on the ballot.

Perhaps you have had a lively conversation with someone of a different generation who sees the world and politics through a lens that doesn't always make sense to you. Perhaps you have had a lively, even difficult, conversation about God, salvation, heaven and hell, and our place in the mix. It doesn't take a statistician to tell us that there is a marked difference in the worldviews of younger and older generations. This difference, along with all the change in society and the world around us, can leave the generations of church members who have served God faithfully for years wondering to whom they will pass the mantle. Whom can they trust to carry on the work of the church and the practices of the kingdom?

Churches across North America have seen a great deal of discontinuity from one generation to the next. As we pick up this story in 2 Kings 2 and see the seamlessness with which one prophet goes on to glory while another puts on the mantle, many of us are left dumb-founded. How can this be so?

Sometimes, when we begin to be convinced by the way of life in the world of kings, we Christians have been all too ready to adopt the story we have been told about young people. Looking at popular culture, we've accepted the idea that young people need to go through a time of searching and "finding themselves," which includes questioning and exploring. We assume it is natural and perhaps even right for young people to leave the church temporarily in order to find themselves. Let's be honest: It can be really frustrating to be around a twenty-year-old who is "figuring things out" and has seemingly rejected everything we hold dear. And perhaps as the church we have been guilty of abandoning them to their self-exploration. Averse to having our authority, practices, and virtues questioned, we let them find answers in a world that will tell them they can be victors, kings, and conquerors just by being themselves. Hopefully, we know that our identity is found in Christ, our selfhood is covered in God's presence, our desires are surrendered to the coming kingdom. But we have no way to speak this word into the lives of young people unless we are willing to be uncomfortable and even disoriented alongside them.

The story of Elijah and Elisha should be quite convincing for a people who seek to make their home in the world of the kingdom and to live according to the patterns of that world. Those patterns go something like this: While generations change, while leaders come and go, the faithfulness of God doesn't leave a faithful people. Young adults do not need to leave the church so long as the church is willing to trust in the faithfulness of God. If we are willing to trust that God will be just as faithful to the next generation as God was to the previous generation, it may do us well to be willing to offer our mantle to the next leaders.

In the story of Elijah and Elisha, it's important to note that Elisha isn't interested in making a name for himself. He isn't trying to draw out the distinctions between himself and the one who came before. Rather, he is far more pleased to be seen as in continuity with Elijah. When Elisha puts on the cloak, you can see that it's the same God who was powerful and mighty through Elijah. Elisha is not looking to build himself a kingdom, to prop up his kind of church or life or politics. In the changing of the guard, God is glorified, not the prophet. And this is entirely different from the way things work in the world of kings.

Some researchers suggest that as many as 90 percent of young people will leave the church after they graduate from high school. As more books, articles, and blogs continue to be written on this dynamic (and there are many), it seems as if a story is being written that suggests that this is simply the way it has to be. But what if the people of God took seriously this continuity issue? We may begin to see a new face under the mantle, but the good news is that we can trust that the mantle is the same and that God's faithfulness will truly endure from generation to generation.

What if we began to be formed so deeply by the patterns of the world of the kingdom that we began to tell a different story ourselves as we live out life together in the church? How much confusion do you think there is between worlds in the church? How often do the patterns of the world of kings come spilling into the life of the church, causing us to measure the story of the church's life according to winners and losers?

But what if our life as the church told the story of the kingdom instead? What if the people of God were so deeply formed by life in the world of the kingdom that they woke up the morning after an election and, no matter what the outcome, were first inclined to offer praise to God for God's faithfulness that has sustained generation after generation and will continue to do so for generations to come? Such an outcome is definitely a possibility for a people who have been deeply formed by the long arc of God's faithfulness through history.

The reality of God's faithfulness will be there four years from now, or four hundred years from now.

THE RECOUNT	
The World of Kings:	**The World of the Kingdom:**
Fears times of change and discontinuity	Sees God's faithfulness from generation to generation
Believes the story is written according to who wins and who loses	Believes the story is written according to God's faithfulness
Considers leaders to be the ones who are able to overpower their opponents	Considers leaders to be the ones upon whom the Spirit of God rests

THE UPSIDE-DOWN HISTORY OF GOD'S KINGDOM

2 KINGS 4:1-7

ON ITS OWN, 2 Kings 4:1-7, the story about the widow and her olive oil, is a fairly inspirational story. Who doesn't love to hear a good underdog story, especially when the underdog wins? But more than sheer inspiration, what is really striking about this story is how subversive it is and how it challenges our notion of kings and kingdoms. It may not appear to be subversive at first, especially when we consider whom we are working with in this story: a financially poor, widowed woman with two sons, nothing in the house to eat, and certainly nothing she can sell to generate an income—except her two sons, into slavery.

STEPPING INTO THE STORY

In the day of this story, selling children into slavery is a last resort, but it does happen. We might think about it like an ancient form of bankruptcy, but with an even more heartbreaking outcome. For those living in ancient Palestine, losing one's children is more than simply the emotional loss; there is also significant financial loss. If we were to think of what direction children take our finances in today, we'd probably be far more likely to think of kids as a drain on our financial resources (even though they are such a blessing!). It's just a simple fact of our society these days: Kids cost us money. There are clothes to buy, food to purchase, educational expenses, and the cost of keeping them involved and entertained, and it all adds up fairly quickly. But in the times of this widow, kids are the retirement plan. They are going to go to work, be productive, and in the family-based society of ancient Palestine, they will contribute their income or their work back to the family.

A widow in this setting would have nothing but her sons to depend on. So when this woman faces the possibility of losing her sons, she also faces the possibility that there will be no one there to claim her, no one there to care for her, to provide for her needs; and, as she ages, she will face the very real possibility of begging for her income.

How, we might ask, can someone in such a desperate situation challenge anything, especially when it comes to the powers of kings and kingdoms? How can someone with no power at all challenge the systems that are the most powerful in her world? How can someone with so little have anything to offer the rest of the world in terms of God's redemptive care and transformative action? In order to understand, we need to back up for a moment and consider the history of Israel and the story of God's salvation woven throughout. Only in this context will we be able to see just how subversive a poor widow can be in a world of kings when the kingdom of God is involved.

We are native Californians, and Tim has a deep affinity for all things related to the splendor of our home state. He's lived near the foothills of the Sierra Nevadas, where he came to appreciate the beauty of the summertime golden, grass-covered knolls dotted with curling and gnarled oak trees against clear blue skies. He also spent seven years living on the shore of the Pacific Ocean, where fresh, cool breezes created a near-perfect climate year round, not to mention the breathtaking magnificence of the places where the surf meets the turf. When it came time to pursue seminary and postgraduate education, we knew we would be leaving behind our native California and moving to a more fickle, Midwestern climate. In those years, we made our home in Kansas City and Chicago—two cities we grew to love. But there's a lot of truth to Dorothy's statement: *There's no place like home.* When people asked what it was like to be from Kansas City or Chicago, we were usually pretty quick to correct them. "We're not *from* Chicago. We're *from* California. Right now, we're temporarily exiled to the Midwest." It was mostly a joke, but there was always a bit of truth in what we said. We missed our home, and—like anyone who has left a place they've loved—we wanted to return one day.

It's that sense of longing for home in the midst of exile that needs to be in the background for us to really understand the story of the widowed mother in 2 Kings 4. Of course, our exile was temporary and, if we're honest, a bit petty. The exile that Israel experiences, the exile in which they are living when 1 and 2 Kings are written, is not guaranteed in their minds to be temporary. Not only are they in exile, but their nation has also been torn in two. For all they know, their situation is permanent, and they are in mourning as a nation.

The division of the kingdom and Israel's exile also probably have a lot to do with *how* they hear this story in light of their own political history and why it is included in 2 Kings. As we all know by now, Israel has a somewhat painful political history. That history began well enough, at the time of the Exodus, escaping from the bonds of slavery and making their way through the wilderness toward becoming their own nation, complete with land, leaders, and a prosperous economy.

During their wilderness wandering, Israel began to learn about faithfulness to the God who brought them out of slavery. Even as they came to recognize that faithfulness would be the foundation of who they were as a people, they struggled with being as faithful to God as God was to them. After many instances and generations of unfaithfulness to God, Yahweh, of course, remained faithful to the covenant and brought Israel into the Promised Land.

Only a few generations later, however, the people began to grow listless and again struggled with the temptation to stop being so unique and chosen, and demanded a king, just like all their neighboring kingdoms had (1 Samuel 8:1-21). Up to that point, the leaders of Israel had been prophets and judges, those who spoke for Yahweh precisely because they had such an intimate knowledge of and openness to God's ways. But Israel opted for something else, a leader who looked more like the kings in the kingdoms they saw around them. "He will take your sons," God warned the people through Samuel, and that was only the beginning of the warnings. In short, God's warning to Israel was that if they wanted a king, they should be prepared to accept that he would lead them from the world of the kingdom into the world of kings, probably without anyone even realizing it. He would do all the things that kings did: war, army conscription, oppressive taxation to support the war and the army conscription, and then, finally, "You yourselves will become his slaves" (1 Samuel 8:17).

Israel received what they asked for. Only two generations after the reign of the great king David, the people of Israel cried out under the oppressive burden of forced labor required of them by Solomon. Solomon's son, Rehoboam, took it to the next level. "My father made your yoke heavy," he told the people; "I will make it even heavier. My father scourged you with whips; I will scourge you with scorpions" (1 Kings 12:14).

All of this was too much to hold the kingdom together. The writer of 1 Kings indicates that upon hearing this, many of the Israelites left the cities that were under the control of Rehoboam. Meanwhile, Jeroboam, an official who had served Solomon but rebelled against him, was hiding in Egypt, waiting for Solomon to die so it would be safe for him to return to his homeland. The political opportunity was there for Jeroboam, and he began to lead those who turned away from Rehoboam, forming a new kingdom. The kingdom, the land, the very identity that God promised Israel, was torn in two, divided against itself. Israel was no longer one; it was now a divided kingdom: Israel and Judah.

So in 2 Kings, when the people of Israel hear a story about a widow with two sons, they can't help but think about the two sons Israel and Judah. Most likely, when they hear the story of the widow who is worried that her sons will be sold into slavery, they think immediately of the two sons Israel and Judah who are on the brink of becoming slaves themselves. Israelite memory has deep scars caused by slavery, and those who hear this story have understood the pain that a mother would endure to watch her sons return to the captivity from which Yahweh promised to free them. At the same time, it's likely that they mourn the fact that Israel and Judah are on the brink of returning to slavery themselves, that the freedom they enjoyed while being faithful to God has been squandered by kings who have been unfaithful to God's commands.

With the background of the history of God's salvation through the people of Israel up to this point, we see that these two sons mean so much more than one woman's retirement plan, or even a mother's affection for her children. These two sons represent the future of the people of God and the divided kingdoms of Israel. With the same audacity with which Jesus compares the kingdom of heaven to a measly mustard seed, 2 Kings compares the future of God's chosen ones with the two doomed sons of a destitute woman. The strange nature of this representation is made more acute when we consider the events of 2 Kings 3, which sets the stage for the story of the widow.

Just before the story of the widow and her sons, we see Judah and Israel trying to work together, like brothers should, only to become the butt of a dark joke. Humor is an important tool in 2 Kings. Who can keep from chuckling a bit when Elisha calls down bears from the woods to eat up a group of teenagers mocking his male pattern baldness (2 Kings 2:23-25)? Second Kings 3 is a tragically humorous story. It opens by telling us who is king and who is becoming king, names that don't mean a whole lot to us today unless we know from

Israel's history that these are not good kings. In fact, they are descended from a long line of kings who have been unfaithful to God, and we begin to see that God's earlier warnings to Israel about their desire for a king weren't baseless.

One of those unfaithful kings of Israel, Joram, decides to collect a debt from the neighboring Moabites. Every good repo man knows to bring backup when you're collecting on a debt. So Joram contacts Jehoshaphat, the king of Judah, the other son. Together, they plot to attack Moab and collect on a debt by capturing their sheep, a valuable commodity and sign of wealth. In order to do this, they will need to pass through the desert region of Edom to get to Moab. They contact the king of Edom, gain his permission to march through his territory, and even promise a bit of their winnings to the Edomite king, so the king of Edom joins their little *Fellowship of the Sheep*. Together, they lay their policy, develop their strategy, and devise their battle plan.

Seven days into their march, however, they begin to realize that attacking through the desert is only a brilliant strategy if you bring water along. But as it turns out, their armies are beginning to dehydrate, and the kings begin to worry that they are going to die before they even reach the border of Moab. "Has Yahweh called us together just to let us die?" Joram asks. His question is a good one, except for this: Yahweh never called them together to begin with. Nowhere in 2 Kings do we see that these kings are acting on some kind of divine directive, or that they even bothered to petition God for assistance. They seem to be assuming that whatever they want to do is God's wish as well. And so, they made their plans, put them into action, and turn to God when they get into trouble.

There are a couple things for us to see here. First, we need to see the contrast between the beginning of the kings' plan with the way the widow begins. Consider the widow's conversation with Elisha and how different it is from what the kings say. "Your servant my husband is dead," the widow says to Elisha, "and you know that he revered the LORD" (2 Kings 4:1). Scholars point out that the woman begins her conversation with Elisha by invoking the name of Yahweh. In other words, she first establishes her request and even her identity as one who is a person of Yahweh. Any request she has for Elisha, anything she says from that point on, is established under God's name.

The coalition of kings, on the other hand, invoke God's name only after their own plans have come to a troublesome impasse. And if you'll notice, Joram even attempts to hang the blame on God for bringing them to the desert. It's a bit comical, it's a bit tragic, but it's also fairly descriptive of the difference between the world of kings and the world of the kingdom.

The good news in the saga of the sheep is that God remains faithful, even in the midst of the Israelite king's unfaithfulness. When the coalition of kings realizes that consulting Yahweh would be a good thing, they begin to inquire about a man of God through whom they can communicate with Yahweh. That man is the one we met in the previous chapter: Elisha. As Elisha sits down with the kings, an interesting exchange takes place. When the kings identify Elisha as one who speaks for God, who is close enough to God and conversant enough with God to open his lips and allow God's words to pour out, Elisha asks them why they want to involve him in their plans to forcibly take sheep from Moab.

At this point, Joram doubles down on his claim that it was Yahweh who brought them to the desert, and it's a claim Elisha can see through immediately. "As surely as the LORD Almighty lives, whom I serve," Elisha responds, "if I did not have respect for the presence of Jehoshaphat king of Judah, I would not pay any attention to you" (2 Kings 3:14). We can almost hear the annoyance in Elisha's voice, perhaps because he recognizes that Joram is still trying to convince others (and perhaps himself) that God brought them to the desert, and now Elisha sees that Joram is trying to get something from God when his own unfaithfulness to God brought him to this place to begin with.

And yet, there is a pivotal point in this exchange because Elisha doesn't completely dismiss Joram. Certainly, Elisha acknowledges Joram's unfaithfulness, but he doesn't allow Joram's side-casting of Yahweh to have the last word. It is a pivot that represents the faithfulness of the God who entered into covenant with Israel, and who is yet again going to remain faithful in the face of unfaithfulness. "This is what the LORD says:" Elisha begins, "I will fill this valley with pools of water" (2 Kings 3:16). And fill the valley God does.

The next morning, water flows in the desert. Perched atop their points of defense, the Moabite army looks down into a valley they have probably seen many times before, a valley that was once a desert but is now covered with liquid that they think to be blood. As the burgundy hues of the sunrise begin to reflect off the water below, the Moabite army is convinced that blood covers the floor of the valley and that the three armies who came to attack them have now turned on one another, spilling their own blood on the valley floor. This is an opportunity unlike anything they have seen, so the members of the Moabite army, rather than return to their homes in peace, run toward the valley in hopes of plundering as much as they can from an unprotected land (2 Kings 3:23). An opportunity turns to terror, however, when they arrive on the scene, only to realize that the armies of aggression are not dead but are simply not as much of early risers as the Moabites. In what follows, the Moabite army is destroyed and driven back to their capital city; in a final act of desperation, the Moabite king takes his son to the wall of the city and sacrifices him for all to see.

Scholars are not in complete agreement about what happens next. The writer of 2 Kings only offers this: "The fury against Israel was great; they withdrew and returned to their own land" (2 Kings 3:27). While we may not be sure about precisely what happens or why exactly Israel isn't victorious, what we are fairly certain of is this: The army of Israel goes home without a single sheep.

There's an additional irony here: Nothing really changes about Israelite history as a result of this military campaign. If this is supposed to be a turning point in the history of Israel's economy, it certainly doesn't accomplish that feat. We get the sense in this story that the king thinks this is going to change something for him and for his kingdom. But at the end of the day, nothing has really changed at all. His campaign is ultimately exposed as a fool's errand, an effort at advancing history that only results in more of the same.

Let's return to the widow with two sons. On the verge of crippling debt and with nothing to sell except her sons, she tells Elisha that she has nothing except a little oil. "Go around and ask all your neighbors for empty jars," Elisha instructs her. "Don't ask for just a few" (2 Kings 4:3). The subtext here is: Get ready to see what happens when God is faithful to those who identify themselves as God's people. It's a good thing the woman asks for more than a few jars. As she pours the oil from her small jar into a larger one, she fills it to the point of overflowing. The same happens with the next. And the next. Every jar in the house is filled, enough to sell in order to pay off her debt, keep her sons, and live on what remains to provide for her family.

If we're looking for this story to advance history in some grandiose way, we're going to be disappointed. A poor woman paying off her debt is not the stuff of history books. No one tells those stories when recounting the way their nation became great—no one, that is, except for God's people, who tell this story as a way of remembering how their history is really made. A kingdom doesn't rise because a woman gets a lot of oil, but the story of God's faithfulness does advance. And God's faithfulness to the poor and powerless is precisely how the history of God's people gets told.

STEPPING INTO THE KINGDOM

Let's not miss the comparison between these stories. On one hand, a group of kings, acting according to the way life operates in the world of kings, makes plans to capture great riches for themselves. They make their own plans, set their own strategy, and act upon them. And when all is said and done, they don't end up with a single sheep. On the other hand, a humble woman with hardly any resources is on the brink of losing everything. She comes to Elisha and only identifies herself under God's name as one of God's people. She seeks nothing more than what she needs, and ends up with more than she could have dreamed.

The point here is not that being part of God's people is a road to riches. Rather, a distinction is being made between the world of kings and the world of the kingdom. As we step into the story of 2 Kings, we begin to *see* differently. We see the way life works in the world of kings, and we see the way life works in the world of the kingdom. The differences between the two give us a different vision of political life than the one we usually have. We see that, though we tend to think history is written by kings going to battle, God's story of salvation is actually being written among those who are on the verge of losing everything. And as we see those alternatives, we are given a choice: Which story do you want to be yours?

That's a question that the writer of 2 Kings wants us to ask as we step into this passage and stand between the story of the kings and the story of the widow. We are meant to examine each one, to measure each according to what it *does* and how each perceives history to be advanced. In that comparison, some questions probably should come to mind: Who wins the battle for the sheep? The kings certainly aren't destroyed, yet they also don't get what they came for. Lives were lost, and for what? Even in the best of circumstances, Israel would return with *some* sheep, adding to what they already have, securing further their own prospects of power and economic prowess because, quite simply, this is what kingdoms do.

History is typically written by the winners of such battles, and the arc of history bends toward the powerful, advanced by those who win battles and turn history toward their plan. But when these stories are held up alongside each other, we begin to see a different reality emerging. It's an upside-down reality that isn't written by highlighting the most powerful or the most wealthy; it is a reality that is written through the stories of God's faithfulness to those who are weak, poor, and vulnerable. It's a history that shines the light of attention on the way God provides for a poor widow to the point of overflowing, and offers salvation for her sons, rather than placing the attention of the story on what warring kings are doing only a few miles away.

While histories of kingdoms are written on the battlefield by those who possess the most military might, the story of God's kingdom is written in places that don't often appear on the map by those who identify themselves not by their ability to take and possess by force but by placing themselves under God's name, and making humble requests precisely because they lack possessions. And the story of God's kingdom is written by the fact that God remains faithful to the least of these. "Don't just ask for a few," Elisha instructs the woman, who sets out in search of jars to hold the oil God will provide. It's more than being hopeful for a supernatural miracle; it's trust in God's faithfulness to the vulnerable, and it's understanding that God's history of salvation is often written in terms of faithfulness to the meek while the powerful do battle a short distance away. For the one who understands history in these terms, she receives to the point of overflowing. To the one who attempts to write history according to his own plans, he leads his army back home with nothing more than he had before. Nothing has changed.

How often do we succumb to the same kind of temptation to begin to set our plans in motion, charge ahead, even building coalitions when necessary, and remember to ask the question about following divine directives only when we get in trouble? We are usually quick to invoke the name of God at the first sign of trouble, to ask for help or direction, perhaps sheepishly attempting to cover the fact that this is the first time in our venture that we are bothering to seek the guidance God has to give, or to ask whether our actions are consistent with the character of God's people.

Political life often has a way of tempting us to act according to the rhythms of life in the world of kings. When it comes to political decisions, the temptation to attempt to bend history according to our desires is a powerful one. We are prone to make our plans, to amass the force necessary to accomplish those plans, and perhaps ask for God's help if we encounter any roadblocks on our way to shaping history. And this is precisely how life works in the world of kings.

One haunting example that comes to mind is that of Union and Confederate soldiers in the American Civil War, kneeling in prayer before battle. Both sides prayed for protection and victory, which are fairly obvious requests, but there was also an underlying theological claim in their prayers: *God is on our side.* In the throes of this bloody military conflict, a minister once remarked to Abraham Lincoln that he hoped God was on his side. "I am not at all concerned about that," came Lincoln's response, "for I know that the Lord is *always* on the side of the *right.* But it is my constant anxiety and prayer that *I* and *this nation* should be on the Lord's *side*."[7] We like Lincoln's theological instincts here, and they differ from those of the three kings we meet in 2 Kings 3. Rather than attempt to begin with God's patterns of actions as revealed to us, we see that the kingly coalition moves ahead with their plans without stopping to consider whether their actions will be faithful to God's ways.

How many times in our own lives do we set plans in motion, only to try to cram God in later, or develop some kind of theological rationale for our actions? Yes, we mean well. Everything we do is for a good cause, like strengthening our city, our state, our country. We are genuinely concerned with making the world a better place. But even the best of intentions have a way of becoming distorted

---

7. Francis Carpenter, *Six Months at the White House with Abraham Lincoln* (Bedford, MA: Applewood Books, 1866), 282.

when they are enacted according to the way life works in the world of kings. Even the best initiative will require us to amass a coalition and go to battle, quickly falling in step with the rhythm of the way life works in the world of kings.

The distinction between the world of kings and the world of the kingdom does not suggest that there is no place in God's kingdom for kings or political leaders. In fact, we ought to be thankful for the kings and political leaders God has given us because those kings recognize that their authority is a derived authority. In other words, kings, rulers, and presidents are to be stewards of what God has entrusted to them, to recognize that they are only authorized to rule with justice, and that their ruling is to be aimed at God's purpose of establishing peace. Rulers—be they kings, presidents, or whatever else—are to be reminded that they are not the ultimate authority but that they serve God's purposes because God is the ultimate authority, mainly because God is good. In the words of Dietrich Bonhoeffer, one of our favorite theologians, "Government has the divine task of preserving the world, with its institutions which are given by God, for the purpose of Christ."[8]

Of course, Bonhoeffer didn't think that every ruler was going to be a fantastic ruler, or submit himself or herself to God's purposes. After all, Bonhoeffer was arrested and executed for his underground work against his own ruler, Adolf Hitler. But Bonhoeffer had a clear sense that if rulers were indeed going to be good rulers, they must first know that they were not the ultimate rulers, and that they served a purpose larger than themselves, given by God, divine in nature. "The mission of government," he wrote, "consists in serving the dominion of Christ on earth by the exercise of the worldly power of the sword and justice."[9] Therefore, those who serve in roles of leader-

---

8. Dietrich Bonhoeffer, *Ethics*, Neville Horton Smith, trans. (New York, Macmillan, 1955), 339.

9. Ibid., 335.

ship of government are to be ministers of God's purposes, to love justice and to do what's good. So political rulers themselves are not the problem. The problem arises when, like the kings in the *Fellowship of the Sheep*, they begin to operate as if they are the ultimate authority.

Bonhoeffer goes on to state that in relationships where there is one person in power or authority, that person is only authorized to execute the powers of his or her office to the degree that the relationship between the two is ordered toward God's goodness. For example, think of a parent and a child. Who has authority in that relationship? Most would claim that the parent has authority. But the child also has authority over the parent inasmuch as they are in relationship with each other. The parent must uphold his or her role, and even authority, rightly if the relationship between parent and child is going to be preserved. The parent has a claim on the child and can discipline the child, instruct the child, and educate the child. But the child also has a claim to make on the parent. The child can call upon the parent to be a parent so that the child can be a child. If the parent does not fulfill his or her role by failing to feed the child, to care for the child, even to discipline the child, the place of authority is lost as the relationship breaks down. Though you may never hear children actually say this, we think they could: "Be a good disciplinarian so we can be well-formed children!" Of course, what we're after here is the idea that parents can't simply use their authority over children in any way they please. There are limits and boundaries to what a parent can and cannot do. When parents use their authority in ways that prevent their children from being well-formed children, we have a word for that: abuse.

A similar claim can be made for rulers and kings. Their position has a purpose: to care for those over whom they rule. If they step beyond those boundaries, or if they fail to fulfill their role, the subjects have a claim to make upon the ruler: "Rule us well so we can be well-formed subjects!" Obviously, Bonhoeffer saw the limits of leadership gravely trespassed in the Nazi regime, and took action against Hitler on the basis that Hitler failed to understand that he was placed in power under God's authority; and, as such, he failed to realize that God, not he, was the final authority. Hitler was confused and mistaken in thinking he could write history, that history could be bent toward his purposes, and that he could use his office to make it so. In fact, history is God's alone.

So yes, there is a place for rulers. Political rulers are not always at odds with the redemptive purposes of God's kingdom, but there are plenty of examples from history in which rulers became confused about whose purposes they were to serve. As we learn in 2 Kings 3, the story of Hitler was an age-old one long before Hitler was ever born. For generations, rulers have been mistaken into thinking they can write history through force and power, and by neglecting their divine purposes of caring for creation until the return of Christ. Perhaps not all, but even the rulers with the best of intentions come to realize at some point that the very systems needed to maintain kingdoms are often at odds with the purposes of the kingdom of God. Kingdoms should be seen for what they are: provisional tools— meant to maintain justice under God's authority until the return of Christ—that are sometimes too clumsy and blunt to be accurate reflections of the kingdom of God.

The temptation for many of us is to imagine that history is written by kings and kingdoms, rather than by the kingdom of God. We are fooled into thinking that history is written by the powerful and faithless, rather than the power of God's faithfulness. We often see that kings and kingdoms are simply the way you "get things done." And, we admit, you can get a lot of things done by making use of the methods of kings and kingdoms. But those things that can be accomplished are quite often a distorted reflection, or a bad copy, of God's redemptive purposes. Our temptation is that we are drawn to the ways and patterns of the world of kings, and because we are so drawn to these things, we forget that these ways can only write a history that is the same kind of cycle of violence we see in 2 Kings 3. It's an old story that has played out across the pages of history time and time again: One kingdom wants what another kingdom has, goes to war, lives are lost, and the goal is ultimately unfulfilled. If we succumb to our temptation to think that history is written this way, this is the history we must be prepared to receive.

On the other hand, an alternative, subversive history is also being written. It's a history of God's faithfulness to redeem even our own unfaithfulness. It's the story of the world of the kingdom of God. It's a history that isn't created by stringing headlines together but, rather, by paying careful attention to the stories of the widows, orphans, and beggars most marginalized and impoverished, and to hear how God has not abandoned them. It's a history that is woven like a thread through all the other histories of kings and kingdoms, yet it is composed of a more sturdy fabric. It's a history that isn't proclaimed from the balconies of majestic towers but is passed from one generation to the next in hushed tones around the campfires of those living in exile.

THE RECOUNT

The World of Kings:	The World of the Kingdom:
Is prone to make plans first and consult God later	Comes under the authority of God, proceeding under God's name
Sees history being written by kings on the battlefield	Sees history being written by God's faithfulness to God's people
Perpetuates the cycle of history that assumes that history is made by winning wars	Can see history advancing through the stories of God's faithfulness to the least of these
Is not always at odds with the purposes of God's kingdom but often struggles to remember that rulers are not the ultimate authority	Is concerned primarily with justice being enacted according to God's redemptive purposes

CLAIMING INVISIBLE POLITICAL OPTIONS

2 KINGS 4:8-37

WE HAVE A STRANGE HISTORY. The people of God have a strange history and a strange way of doing life that rarely makes sense in the world of kings. In the previous chapter, we saw how strange our history is. It's not only told in strange ways, but it also advances in strange ways. We saw how, while the kings fought battles, doing what their kingdoms expected them to do, they gained nothing and changed nothing. The strange history of God's people unfolds as a powerless widow was given more than enough oil to save her sons. Unlike the kings who went to battle for sheep and gained nothing, she gained much, to the point of overflowing. The history of God's faithfulness unfolds in strange, upside-down ways.

STEPPING INTO THE STORY

The passage in 2 Kings 4:8-37 tells us another part of our strange history. There are certainly peculiar components to this story, but it's more that the whole message of this story is a strange way of seeing the world from a political and economic standpoint. Much like the story we examined in the last chapter, this is yet another story of a mother and a son. This time, we meet not a poor widow but a woman from Shunem who is economically well off, married to a man who has provided for her needs. That provision is about to run out, however. The woman's husband is elderly, and as the story begins, we learn that she has no son. In the ancient world, a woman without a husband or a son is in an unspeakably tough economic position. The societal norms of the day mandate that a woman not work, so women depend on husbands and sons to meet the needs of everyday life. In the case of the Shunammite woman in 2 Kings 4, her husband's days are numbered—and so is her provision.

From the time we first meet this woman, we get the sense that there is something different about her vision. When she sees Elisha passing through her hometown, she immediately identifies him as a holy man of God. We're not told if there are any identifying markers about Elisha that set him apart as a prophet on that particular day—and that may be the point. What we encounter here is a woman who can see things rightly. Whereas others may see a drifter, a political operative, or even a lunatic, she sees Elisha as a holy man of God. We get an immediate sense that she can see what others can't.

It is with that vision that the woman not only offers Elisha a meal but goes so far as to have a guest room built for him at her house so he will have somewhere to stay whenever he is passing through the area. In other words, the woman extends some incredibly generous hospitality to Elisha. There's nothing in the story that suggests she does so because she thinks she can get something from Elisha. Instead, we're led to believe that her act of welcome is out of sheer generosity of spirit. Nevertheless, Elisha wants to give her something back—something she has never asked for.

Quite frankly, the offer is something we probably wouldn't expect from Elisha. "Can we speak on your behalf to the king or the commander of the army?" (2 Kings 4:13). We need to remember where Elisha has just been. In the war of blunders executed by the *Fellowship of the Sheep* (could we call it Sheepgate?) and recorded in

2 Kings 3, the kings called upon Elisha to give them counsel, and as it turned out, his advice was really pretty good. Elisha, then, is an advisor to the most powerful and connected men in the country. He has their ear, and they listen to him. A recommendation from Elisha would likely go a long way.

We're not told clearly what kind of recommendation this would be, but it's reasonable to assume, because of the woman's aging husband, that there may be marital undertones to Elisha's potential commendation of the woman to the king. Because marriage is the way to economic security for women in Elisha's time, it's not outside the realm of possibility that Elisha might be suggesting he set the woman up with the king in hopes that the king will take her as a wife after the woman's husband dies.

The king we're talking about here is Joram, the same king we met in 2 Kings 3, the king who went to war for sheep and came home empty-handed. The writer of 2 Kings isn't Joram's biggest fan. "He did evil in the eyes of the LORD," we are told in 3:2. Perhaps this is why the woman responds to Elisha's offer the way she does.

"I have a home among my own people," she tells the prophet (2 Kings 4:13). At first glance, her response is confusing. As a resident of Shunem, this woman is almost certainly an Israelite, a subject of the king of Israel, Joram. Yet the woman seems to see some kind of gulf between them; her response points to a sense of disconnection, that she doesn't think she is actually one of Joram's people. An answer that seems simple on the surface begins to take on more complexity when you see how carefully the woman has phrased her response. She hasn't said anything pejorative about the king, but neither has she given the slightest hint that she is interested in leaving her situation and entering into the king's world. It could be that she refers to her own community, her local town of Shunem, but there may also be a sense in which this woman is showing that she sees things differently, that she can see an alternative world with an alternative set of political possibilities.

There are two political possibilities the woman has, just as we all have. She can accept the political world as it's given to her, the world of kings, or she can opt for an alternative way, the world of the kingdom. The world of kings is the world of politics as we most readily know it. It comes to us with its systems already intact, especially systems of power and economic might. It usually tells us that the way to economic security is to get as close as we can to whomever happens to have the power. Sometimes it even tells us we need to do whatever we can to get close to power. Most of the time, it also suggests that any hope we have for economic security will be found in what it—the world of kings—can provide.

The world of the kingdom, on the other hand, unfolds in the strange history of God's people. It often wants to suggest to us not merely an alternative political system that is meant to compete with all the other political systems in the world of kings; rather, it wants to suggest an alternative political world altogether, with options that are not available in the world of kings. The world of the kingdom is one we can begin to see with the eyes of the Shunammite woman.

In this particular case, the world of kings would tell this woman that if she is going to be cared for, she ought to take advantage of this windfall of fortune. After all, Elisha is an advisor to the king, and the king listens to him. In the world of kings, you take advantage of situations like that. You make the most of them when they come because they don't come around all that often. Yet we've already begun to sense that this woman wants to operate in a different political world entirely. When she first sees Elisha, he is not the king's advisor to be exploited but a holy man of God to be welcomed. When given the option, then, of being commended to the king, she declines, suggesting that while Joram lives in the world of kings, she opts to live in the world of the kingdom.

Old Testament scholar Walter Brueggemann is helpful in shedding more light on this point. When he reflects on this passage and on 2 Kings in general, he describes it as a "testimony to otherwise."

Otherwise is the name Brueggemann ascribes to the possibilities given to the people of God that are not always readily available in the world of kings. Brueggemann suggests that imagination, or the ability to see a world other than the world as it is given to us, is part of the good news being communicated to us through the narrative of 2 Kings. Like the Shunammite woman, God's people are given an ability to see and imagine an alternative world, an ability "increasingly recognized and valued as a way in which we are led and transformed by God's category-shattering, world-forming spirit."[10] In the case of the Shunammite, she is offered the category of the given political world. She is offered the chance to cozy up to power for her own benefit, something that isn't strange or out of place in the given world of kings. But she sees another way. In Brueggemann's words, she employs "the God-given, emancipated capacity to picture (or image) reality—God, world, self—in alternative ways outside conventional, commonly accepted givens."[11]

"I have a home among my own people" becomes a response of someone who can see another way, a way consistent with the world of the kingdom. In the world that the woman can see, she doesn't need to be commended to the king to know that her future is secure, especially when the king in question is one who is so prone to occupy the world of kings that he will go to war to amass wealth, gain nothing, and then return to the business of attempting to maintain political power. The woman's people might be the residents of Shunem, but more fully, the woman's people are the ones who can envision a political world that isn't based on the logic and rhythms of the world of kings.

The witness of the Shunammite woman is challenging to those of us who have had our own political vision and imagination formed by the political world as it is given to us. Often, we take the political

---

10. Walter Brueggemann, *Testimony to Otherwise: The Witness of Elijah and Elisha* (St. Louis: Chalice Press, 2001), 27.

11. Ibid.

world for granted. We think this is simply the way things are and that we must either take this world on its own terms or be excluded altogether. Coming from an American context, we see this to some extent in the dominant two-party system. In that given political context, we've learned that you generally need to choose one party or the other, align yourself with that party's platform, and oppose the other party's approach entirely. The choices are given to you, and you rarely get to choose a viable option that isn't already on the table. The given world of the American two-party political system is part of what the witness of the Shunammite woman challenges in us, but there is a larger concept at work here. Moreover, her witness challenges the larger logic of the world of kings and the way that world operates according to the need to control the world by gaining power.

The world of kings is built on the logic of using power against the opposition to gain as much control as possible. The drive for power and control compels the entire political enterprise in the world of kings. The given political world of kings begins with the attempt to gain power and ends with the attempt to gain power. Brueggemann puts it like this: "Because of the endless pressure and the insatiable need to control, it is our human wont to establish a fixed, visible, settled 'given' that is beyond criticism or reexamination, a 'given' that variously partakes of intellectual, socioeconomic, political, and believing components."[12] Part of being human, Brueggemann suggests, is a desire to control our circumstances, and we tend to attempt to control things according to the logic of the world as it is given to us. If we see that the world works according to the logic of winners and losers, we strive to be one of the winners through the mechanisms that make winners. We rarely stop to question the underlying logic of the entire system of making winners and losers.

---

12. Brueggemann, *Testimony to Otherwise,* 27.

Elisha's offer to put in a good word with the king on behalf of the woman is a puzzling suggestion that she simply play the game according to the rules that have been given to her, but she chooses to propose a different rulebook. According to the logic of the world of kings, the woman has just condemned herself to a life of miserable poverty and destitution. Only the king can save her because, in the logic of the world of kings, the king is the winner. "I have a home among my own people" becomes a subversion of the world of kings. It does not seek to tear down the world of kings, or even criticize it. Rather, her response simply states that she'd prefer not to live according to its logic. She will live among her own people, and she will let the king do what kings do, but she won't be persuaded to choose between the options as they are presented to her. Nor will she live into the suggestion that the king and his political world are the source of her hope. This is a woman who sees a holy man of God rather than a politically connected operative, a woman who has hope in the world of the kingdom rather than in the king's power.

Even considering the woman's response, we must admit that Elisha's offer itself is perplexing. Why would he offer her a deeper level of participation in the world of kings? Perhaps this is a way of Elisha testing her. It might be that he wants to know whether that offer is appealing to her as a gauge of her hope in the power and political might of the world of kings. Or, maybe Elisha can't see for himself how deeply he has been formed by the given political world and needs the witness of the woman's perspective to help him see an alternative. Whatever Elisha's reasoning, the point here is that we ought to be challenged by the Shunammite woman's witness and her ability to see things that others can't. In the world of the kingdom, she needn't ally herself with a man who has a lot of power because God will be her salvation.

Everything about the woman's words and actions suggest that she has simply been so deeply formed to hope in the world of the kingdom that she is capable of seeing that she doesn't need to enter into the 'this or that' of the world of kings. For her, it is not get close to power or die in destitution. Rather, she rejects both options in favor of choosing the option no one else seems able to see: hoping in God for her salvation. The story of God's people is a strange one, indeed.

We shouldn't forget that the writer of 2 Kings includes this story in contrast to the narrative of the kings who, according to the logic of the world of kings, go to battle for sheep. By setting up this contrast, the writer is asking an implicit question: Where will God's story be written? The logic of the given political world—the world of kings—tells us that history is written by people in positions of power whose names will be remembered for generations. But we shouldn't overlook the fact that the Shunammite woman is never named. She is nameless and powerless—a curse, if she were attempting to live according to the world of kings. But, as one who opts to populate the world of the kingdom, she is remembered by us as a saint, as one whose faith challenges our own, and as a woman who can see an alternative to the political world as it is given to her. Thus, the political benefit of what the king might have to offer isn't necessarily of great hope to her. A son, however, would be a different story.

As we already know, Elisha wants to do something to repay the kindness of the Shunammite woman for her hospitality. She has already declined his offer to put in a good word for her with the king, but Elisha doesn't want to give up. "What can be done for her?" he asks Gehazi, his servant (2 Kings 4:14).

At this point Gehazi reminds Elisha of this woman's true predicament. "She has no son, and her husband is old" (2 Kings 4:14).

That is exactly the information Elisha needs. He signals for the woman to come to him, and he gives her something no king could ever provide. He tells her that within a year, she will hold a son in her arms. It is clearly something only God can provide. But it is also a strange imposition on the woman because, if she will receive this gift, it requires that she take hold of something very dangerous. She must take hold of hope. That is something this woman is not prepared for. We don't know if Elisha knows what he is asking of her in attempting to give her this gift because the woman's reaction is so stringently against what Elisha suggests. If we thought she was resolute in turning down Elisha's first offer, we see just how strong she can be when she turns down this one. "'No, my lord!' she objected" (2 Kings 4:15).

If it seems strange that a woman with no retirement plan is turning down the offer of a gift that would be the modern equivalent of a fully funded 401(k), perhaps we ought to remember what this gift really is: It is hope. It isn't that the woman doesn't want to have a son. It is that she doesn't want to live in hope if that hope is never going to be realized. "Please, man of God, don't mislead your servant" (2 Kings 4:15).

If Elisha's promise turns out to be true, it will change the trajectory of the rest of her days on earth. It will mean provision rather than destitution. It will mean she'll retire comfortably rather than turn to life on the streets. But it is a big *if*, and that is more than the woman can bear. It's almost as if the woman is saying, "I can't take that. I can take the fact that my husband is old, that he's going to die and leave me to beg on the streets. I've accepted that. I've made my peace with my situation. But please don't dangle hope in front of me. I can't deal with taking hold of hope, only to have it crushed. So please don't ask me to hope for something that can never be."

It's intriguing to wonder whether Elisha knows what he is offering her. Maybe he considers it a great gift, an act of returning hospitality. But perhaps he doesn't realize how much this gift will demand from the woman at the same time. A son would be a profound gift, but even the *idea* of having a son of her own requires that she take hold of hope, and to stop making peace with her situation. Rather than the comfortable—if depressing—pattern of knowing what is coming her way, the very concept of having a son requires that hope be awakened within her.

Anyone who has ever gone to a job interview has probably thought at least a little bit about how different life would be if they could just get that job. Anyone who has been offered the possibility of a different work situation, a better schedule, a more loving work environment, maybe even a higher salary, has probably taken hold of a little bit of hope. But anyone who has ever been turned down for a job after the interview probably knows the feeling of wishing they'd never had the interview to begin with. The same is probably true of the Shunammite woman. If there were some guarantee that this son Elisha talks about would be born, hope would be a welcome arrival. In the absence of that guarantee, however, hope is a dangerous and fickle companion.

We are no strangers to this feeling. None of us is untouched by hopes that have gone unrealized, but personally, as pastors, we come into contact with a host of unrealized hopes, especially in the lives of our people. We serve a wonderful congregation of people who are not strangers to the unrealized hope of being able to have children— by miscarriages, by the loss of lives that ended far too soon, by jobs that disappear. There's something about hope that takes root deep in our souls, and when it's taken from us, many of us wish we had never hoped at all rather than have that hope taken away.

It's helpful to remember that 2 Kings was written at a time when the people of Israel are experiencing a crisis of hope. The book of 2 Kings comes to be assembled into a written form while they are exiled from the land and homes that have been promised to them. After having experienced the joy of having a place of their own, it has all been taken from them, and they are once again a people in exile. They are now a people without a country, without a king, without a kingdom. The political world of kings does not protect them from captivity. Rather, it was a king and his army who overcame them both politically and militarily, and any hope they placed in the world of kings has now disappeared. The hopes for being a people based on the logic of the world of kings has faded, and now they begin to remember just how strange the history of God's story is. It is beginning to dawn on them that the political logic of the kingdom could be real to them when the world of kings has left them abandoned. They now live in a foreign land as strangers and outsiders, and there is no foreseeable end to this arrangement. They might be a people in exile forever; there is no guarantee that they will ever get to go home. It could very well be the case that, as they assemble these particular stories from their own strange history, they are asking themselves, *Is this just the way it's going to be from now on? Should we stop hoping for something more than this? Is this simply the way the world works? Should we just learn to deal with it?* Hope can be painful.

Despite the woman's protests to Elisha, she does bear a son within the year. As she holds that son in her arms, she embraces the hope of a good future. As the story tells us, the baby grows to be old enough to help in the fields, exactly what the woman needs the boy to do if he is going to fulfill the promise of her hope. As he works in the fields one day, he begins to complain that his head hurts. He tells his father, and—like any good dad—his father instructs the boy to go tell his mother. When the boy arrives home, complaining to his mother about the pain in his head, she takes him into the room she built for Elisha. She holds him in her lap, and, just as she did when he was first born, she literally hangs on to the promise of hope.

And her son dies.

The thing about hope is this: When you don't have it, it's easy to forget about it. You don't have to care because you don't have to feel anything because you weren't expecting a different outcome. But once you have it, once you let yourself get swept away in the possibility of what might be, once you allow yourself to really, truly hope, it's unbearable to lose. This mother is probably experiencing that. She held on to hope. She didn't ask for it; it was given to her. And now, she cannot bear the thought of losing it.

Immediately after her son's death, the Shunammite woman goes out to find Elisha, the man of God. Perhaps she can't accept the fact that this situation is real, but it probably has something more to do with knowing how she might be able to recover hope. Again, we are probably catching a glimpse of how differently this woman happens to see the world. She knows where hope can be found.

She sets out to find Elisha, and as Elisha sees her coming, he sends out Gehazi, his servant, to ask the woman if everything is all right. When he does ask, the woman lies to him. "Everything is all right" (2 Kings 4:26). We are tempted to think her response might be something she utters in faith, claiming that everything *will* be all right once the man of God gets involved, but there seems to be something a little more raw and desperate in her response. Bypassing Gehazi, the woman clings to Elisha's feet as she cries. "'Did I ask you for a son, my lord?' she said. 'Didn't I tell you, "Don't raise my hopes"?'" (2 Kings 4:28). Elisha knows what's wrong. Immediately, he sends Gehazi to do something about the situation, giving Gehazi his staff, which represents Elisha's presence.

But before Gehazi can leave, the woman says an interesting thing: "As surely as the LORD lives and as you live, I will not leave you" (2 Kings 4:30). If you've read through 2 Kings, this probably rings a bell. That's because it's a direct quote from 2 Kings 2:2. Elisha himself said the very same thing to Elijah when he was asking to become a son of a man of God. Elisha understands what's behind these words, so he goes with the woman.

Gehazi arrives at the woman's house first. Taking Elisha's staff, he lays it against the boy's face, and the boy remains dead. In this case, Gehazi acts as a proxy for Elisha, a delegate dispatched to represent the man himself. But there are some tasks for which a proxy simply will not do. Elisha arrives, and we come to see just how strange this story gets.

Going into the room, he takes a moment to pray then climbs on top of the dead boy, "mouth to mouth, eyes to eyes, hands to hands" (2 Kings 4:34). Of course this is strange, and if we're honest, it makes us uncomfortable in at least a couple of ways. The point here is that there is nothing between Elisha and the boy. A delegate—a go-between—would not do, so now there is nothing between the man of

God and the dead hopes of a nameless woman who chose not to trust her future to the king but to the kingdom. Elisha is bringing the full presence of God to bear on the body of this child.

As he does, the boy's body returns to life. In a strangely playful description of what takes place next, the boy sneezes seven times. Hebrew, the language in which 2 Kings is written, can be a little slippery at points, so what we translate as "sneeze" could possibly be a gasp or some other kind of respiratory reflex, but the point is that the boy who was dead, and the hope that died with him, is now alive. He is sneezing, and he is blinking. When the Shunammite woman responds to Elisha's summons, she sees her son alive and falls down to the ground in an act of thankful humility. Then she takes her son and leaves.

STEPPING INTO THE KINGDOM

This story, in many ways, is uncomfortably physical. It's very real. The idea of being hand to hand, eye to eye, and mouth to mouth sets us on edge because of how physical it is. Some of the most real physical realities we face are birth and death, both of which are present in this story. Birth and death are physical realities that no living person can escape, and in some sense, that tends to make us uncomfortable. Very few people we know are totally comfortable with either process.

For generations, a discomfort with the physical realities of life has led humans to make a fairly strong distinction between things that are physical and things that are spiritual. Even before Jesus, Greek philosophers based their view of the world on a two-tier reality: the spiritual reality and the physical reality. One philosopher in particular, Plato, was very uncomfortable talking about a fusion of spiritual and physical, rejecting the possibility that the spiritual could touch the physical, and arguing that a distinction between the two must be maintained.

Though this penchant for separating physical from spiritual wasn't a particularly strong influence on those who penned the Old

Testament, it has most certainly influenced Christian believers, almost from the beginning of the church's existence. One strand of early Christian belief, called Gnosticism—ultimately rejected by the church—maintained that Jesus couldn't have been both truly human and truly divine because, according to their belief, spiritual and physical realities can't touch. These Gnostic influences haven't left us entirely. We still struggle on a regular basis with the temptation to understand spiritual realities as totally separate and other from physical realities. When we talk about the kingdoms of this world and the kingdom of God, it's awfully easy for us to assume the same distinction, and to believe that the kingdoms of this world get all the physical stuff. They get things like our bodies and our money and our votes and our money and more of our money. The very physical realities of birth and death are certified by the state in most cases, and those records are housed by governmental authorities; the world of the king holds the records of our births and the records of our deaths. The kingdom of God, on the other hand, gets all of our spiritual stuff, like our love and devotion and commitment and faith and our hope, because all of that is not quite as real, physical, or certifiable.

Philosophical distinctions between spiritual and physical might seem fairly innocuous in a political sense until we begin to talk about hope. If the spiritual realities of the world really have nothing to do with the physical realities of the world, where do you place your hope? In many ways, the world of kings would tell us that if you want economic security, you don't have an option for the political placement of hope. You must place your hope in the world of kings, which means your king must be the strongest, your kingdom must be the largest, and when your king goes to battle for sheep, he must come home with more than he started with.

If our hope is placed in the world of kings, along with its distinction between spiritual and physical realities, an insidious dismantling of that hope often follows; despair begins to seep in where our hope has been fractured. In 2008, the United States was ramping up for a presidential election, the economy was unraveling at the seams, and many people were on the brink of unemployment and bankruptcy, so the concept of hope played well to an electorate who were generally convinced of the separation between the real and the spiritual. When the real things of life have been given over to the world of kings, our only option is to place hope in the king. The problem was that, a mere four years later, a great deal of the American electorate had begun to lose faith in the governmental structure that had promised hope. And yet, in light of the given political options, many Americans simply attempted to place their hope in the other guy who might do for them what they wanted.

Of course, the 2012 presidential election was a closer contest than 2008, which was somewhat telling about the American vision of hope: We continued to believe that the person in office could restore our hope. The problem is that as long as we place our hope in the world of kings, with its assumed distinction between physical and spiritual realities, we will always be disappointed to some extent. Placing hope in the world of kings will never be able to fully satisfy what we truly long for because the world of kings operates according to the premise that it has everything that is real and that it alone has the ability to provide real things, real money, real security, and real hope.

Here's the problem with the basic assumptions underlying the world of kings: Real stuff has never been the exclusive possession of kings. God has always worked with real stuff. The God of the Shunammite woman is the God who worked with the real stuff of the primordial creation, who separated the land and water and the light and dark and the day and night, who knit us together in our mothers' wombs and who ultimately participated in and experienced the physical realities of birth and death through the incarnation of Jesus. God works in physical things like water, wine, and bread. However we might attempt to divide up spiritual from physical realities, those divisions have never accurately reflected the way God has worked to create and redeem the world. The exclusive assignment of physical realities to the world of kings is inconsistent with the salvation history of God.

But as long as we live in a world that is separated, as long as we understand real stuff to be different from spiritual stuff, we are tempted to think that God doesn't handle real stuff, and to assign our hope to the world of kings. Real stuff is given over to the kingdoms of this world, and God, we are led to believe, will handle the spiritual side of things. Even though time and time again in Scripture we see God dealing with real stuff like birth and life and death, and even though we continue to witness God's faithfulness in the midst of real stuff, we are prone to be a people who functionally separate out God's faithfulness with the real stuff of life from the political realities of our world.

If we are to follow the suggestion that the world is divided between spiritual and physical, despair is only a short step away. If we believe that the world of kings has primary possession over all that is real while the world of the kingdom takes charge only over that which is spiritual, ethereal, and evanescent, we will come face to face with the reality that the world of kings is not capable of providing the fullness of what we need to be human. When we place our hope in the world of kings and watch as our king returns from battle with no more sheep than he had before, despair closes in like a shadow.

Sometimes this separation, this ripping apart of our hope, is what causes us to get really hot-headed about things like elections. As long as we think in terms of separation, we will ultimately believe that political entities and governmental forces are the ones who have control of the real stuff. We become anxious because we think the kingdoms of this world have control over the physical things, and we only trust God with the spiritual stuff. In the same way that Israel experienced the despair and anxiety of a lost kingdom, we become a divided people who cling to the notion that the only way to ward off despair is to place our hope in the ability of the next politician or king to bring home sheep. And too often, when the king returns home, there are no sheep to be seen.

Whereas the initial readers of 2 Kings might understand the world to be a divided place, a severed reality demanding that we place our hope in our king's ability to be stronger than the neighboring king to meet our physical needs, the Shunammite woman seems to be able to see something different. It is the world of the kingdom in which "the cattle on a thousand hills" belong to the God who "created the heavens and the earth" (Psalm 50:10, Genesis 1:1). The death of the Shunammite woman's son does not open the way to despair precisely because she clearly sees that she has a home among her own people and that she does not need to give herself to the world of kings to be able to have hope.

The Shunammite woman's witness is one that brings political unity to the world, drawing together the physical and spiritual realities of the world under her trust in God's faithful provision, and her ability to see another political way that does not require placing her trust solely in the way of the king. As the Shunammite woman decides to run to Elisha rather than the king, she pulls together the fabric of a divided world. She will not leave until God has done a work in her life to restore hope.

Terence Fretheim, a renowned Old Testament scholar, has reflected on the story of the Shunammite woman and her witness that challenges our assumptions of a divided world. "This is not escapist literature, designed to take one out of the world; rather, it puts life back into place according to God's creational design, and throws these people back into their everyday world."[13] In other words, the Shunammite's testimony demonstrates the way of the kingdom, which includes the understanding that God is not looking to separate the believers out of this world. Nor are we meant to accept that

---

13. Terence E. Fretheim, *First and Second Kings* (Lousiville: Westminster John Knox Press, 1999), 149.

this is simply going to be the way the world is. Instead, we are meant to be the kind of people who, as part of the real stuff of creation, are used by God for redemptive purposes in the world, even when that means turning the world's assumptions about political hope upside down. Hope in the kingdom of God alters reality. It isn't the kind of hope we might find in a kid waiting up on Christmas Eve, thinking, *I really hope I get that game I want.* For Christians, hope is leaning into the promises of God. Leaning indicates both motion and dependence. Christian hope takes seriously the promises of God.

What if Christians were to stop living as a divided people? What if we were to trust in God with our whole selves? What would it be like to live like God if Christians who really believe in things like God's provision in the midst of difficult circumstances started opening homes for unwed mothers and opening their own homes to fostering and adopting children? What if Christians who felt passionate about issues like the national debt began to get their own personal debt under control so they could live as generous people? What if Jesus wasn't under house arrest in our hearts and was truly on the move in and through our actions?

Hope is really powerful. If you dare to put your hope in God, rather than in the world of kings, you will not despair. A couple hundred years after the Shunammite woman, the people of Israel find themselves being ruled by yet another oppressive king. And yet again, they begin to ask themselves, *Is this just the way it has to be? Is this just the way the world works?* And in the midst of their darkest hour, God sends a Son who is incarnated of the real stuff of life. And when that Son meets the physical reality of death, and just when his followers look upon his body hanging from an execution device with strong political overtones and hang their heads and say, "I guess this is just the way the world works"—at their lowest moment—God is already loosening the graveclothes and rolling away the stone. In the resurrection of Jesus, God breaks the power that suggests that physical reality has ultimate power over us. Christ has conquered death, the ultimate physical reality. It is real, yes, but it is no longer in a place of ultimate authority. Hope in God, and you will not despair.

The narratives of 2 Kings do not assume a stark distinction between physical and spiritual realities, and they challenge us to follow suit. While Joram may assume that the world of kings is simply the way things work, while he may assume that if his subjects are to have hope, they must place that hope in his abilities to be a powerful king, the Shunammite woman sees a political alternative. Rather than placing her hope in the world of kings, she places it in the world of the kingdom. Had she chosen another route, had she accepted Elisha's offer and hoped in what the king might be able to provide, history would probably have overlooked the Shunammite woman because she would likely have fallen to despair when her greatest hopes were not realized. But in a political sense, she places her hope in the world of the kingdom, in a God who remains faithful to the people of Israel, even when Israelite kings are anything but faithful.

In her witness, we find ourselves challenged to examine where we have placed our hope. If our hope is in the world of kings, it makes every bit of sense that we would go to political war with one another, because the world of kings will be our provider. But if we can follow the faithful lead of a nameless woman through whom God wrote another chapter in the saga of salvation history, our response to the temptation to join the world of kings may be something more closely aligned with, "I have a home among my own people." Should we join her in this refrain, we may be able to see a political alternative, an "otherwise" that cannot be offered to us by the world of kings, and as we do so, we may just find that a fractured hope unto despair can be knit together once again as we step into the world of the kingdom.

THE RECOUNT

The World of Kings:	The World of the Kingdom:
Assumes a divide between physical and spiritual realities	Assumes that all the world belongs to God, the creator of heaven and earth
Finds hope in making the right associations with politically connected and powerful people	Finds hope in God's long history of being faithful to God's people
Operates according to a limited set of political options based in opposition	Operates according to a set of political options that cannot always be seen by the world of kings
Has the potential to perpetuate the back-and-forth of oppositional political life	Has the potential to enact options that rise above the back-and-forth of oppositional political life

POLITICAL ENGAGEMENT AND FAITHFUL LIVING

2 KINGS 4:38-41

IN 2 KINGS 4:38-41, there is a story of Elisha fixing a cooking error that has caused a meal to go horribly awry. This particular story reminds us of a cooking adventure from early in our marriage. Tim grew up in a household that did a lot of cooking, so when we got married, Tim just assumed he had more experience and would do a lot of the cooking. The problem was that we have very different philosophies of food. For Tim, food is simply a necessity. We need to eat. Sometimes what we eat needs to be heated. Sometimes all we need to do is open a can and put a spoon in it.

Shawna, on the other hand, wants food to be an experience. For her, a meal is like a finely composed symphony. Each course should be like a different movement, one building upon the next, themes and motifs intertwining, rewarding those who give the most attention to the subtleties of the art. One flavor should complement another, and they should flow together in nuanced and delicate ways, making what Tim thought was simple nutrition a thing of intricate beauty.

Once we realized how different our philosophies were, we agreed that Shawna would do more of the cooking in our house. When we had been married only a few months, Shawna called Tim and told him she had discovered a new recipe for a broccoli salad, and that if at all possible, he should get home early because this was going to be a treat no one should miss. Tim wrapped up things at the office and got home as soon as he could to experience Shawna's latest work of art. In any art, however, an artist should know the media well. As it happened, two cloves of garlic were a foreign medium of that evening's culinary pursuit. Shawna did not know the difference between a clove and a bulb of garlic. Doing what she believed the recipe called for, Shawna diced nearly eight times the amount of garlic that she should have and added it to the main course.

On that particular night in our household, there was death in the pot.

STEPPING INTO THE STORY

In many ways, 2 Kings 4 is like a story valley. On one side, you have the mountain of a story that records a great battle between the team of Israel, Judah, and Edom against the team of Moab. On the other side is the mountain of a story about Naaman, who is "commander of the army of the king of Aram" as well as "a valiant soldier" (5:1). Chapters 5 and 6 go on to describe the war between Israel and the Arameans. But chapter 4, the valley between these two mountains, is a chapter about those who have very little, those who represent some of the weakest of Israelite society, those without resource or hope. We've already seen that chapter 4 is loaded with all kinds of stories of God's faithfulness to those in incredible need. A widow caring for her family, a woman who dares to hope, and people who are hungry are the characters who show up here. But chapter 4 is really interesting to us because of its surroundings. Chapters 3 and 5 are totally different from chapter 4 because 3 and 5 are both stories about powerful political rulers.

There are even some interesting signs on your way in and out of the valley of chapter 4, marking the boundaries. The first verse contains a direct reference to God's proper name, Yahweh, as does the last verse (4:1, 4:44). In our Bibles, we probably see the word LORD show up in these verses, but every time we see LORD in small capital letters, it means that the original writers of these stories, who wrote in Hebrew, used God's proper name, which we translate into English as *Yahweh*. For those of us who speak English, we really only have one word for God, and sometimes we use it in a generic sense, and other times we use it to refer to the specific God of Abraham, Isaac, and Jacob. But in Hebrew, there are several words that could be used for God, and often, the use of God's proper name means serious business. It carries more weight. It is so revered and treated with such respect that a special pen was used just to write it.

So the fact that this name bookends this collection of underdog stories should tell us something. As we read through 2 Kings 4, we are given a signal that we are entering Yahweh's territory on the way in, and being reminded that we have been in Yahweh's territory on the way out. When you enter Yahweh's territory, you start to see that things are different. In Yahweh's territory, history is not written by the powerful on the mountains but by the faithful in the valley. In Yahweh's territory, those who are poor find that there is enough. In Yahweh's territory, those who are most vulnerable are those God uses to be blessings to others.

The appearance of the story valley stands out as a reminder of what is taking place in the life of Israel as these stories are being assembled. As the writer knows, the meaning and message sometimes come across not only in the story itself but in its juxtaposition with another story, so that we can clearly see that one of these things is not like the other. A story valley would come as good news to the people of Israel. As this collection of stories of God's faithfulness is being ascribed to parchment, Israel is living in exile. They are living in the rubble of a crushing military defeat that has left them homeless and hopeless. Their sons have been taken from them, likely conscripted into Babylonian military service or slave labor, and as a nation, they are on the verge of losing their identity. In essence, Israel would easily identify with valley people—those walking through the lowest point between two mountains.

In these stories—in remembering them and telling them and writing them—Israel begins to recover much of what was lost when they were forcibly exiled from their land. Even when their sons—their hope for the future of their national identity—are taken from them, they evoke the story of God's faithfulness to those who were close to losing their identities, and in remembering these accounts, they also remember that they are God's people. The stories they tell shape who they are, how they talk, and even how they think. These are stories that make them a unique people, a people with a different way of life that is deeply impacted by the faithfulness of Yahweh. In other words, they are the stories that mark out what life is like for those who live in Yahweh's valley. To be people of the valley means that the valley stories mark the kind of people we are. And what kinds of things happen in the valley? Widows are cared for. People are given hope. Things that were thought to be useless and beyond redemption are healed, redeemed, and enlisted for God's purposes.

One of the valley stories of chapter 4 relates Elisha doing a little cooking. It's one of the stranger stories in 2 Kings 4, but it has something to teach us about political engagement as God's people. In this narrative, Elisha returns to Gilgal, an area that has been distressed by a famine. While gathered together with several other prophets, they realize that their normal supply of food isn't available, which leaves them to gather what they can find and get creative. Whatever herbs and vegetables can be found will become the evening meal. When all is said and done, the meal probably should be delicious. After all, it is a stewed collection of native plants and vegetables mixed together with some seasoning. It almost makes us hungry just thinking about it. But sadly, something goes wrong. Some of the gourds that Elisha's servant found are inedible, either because they taste horrible, or they are outright poisonous. "There is death in the pot!" they exclaim, perhaps a bit dramatically (2 Kings 4:40). Maybe the concoction really is deadly. Or maybe they are just having fun with a friend who turns out to be a terrible cook. Either way, no one is eating it. Elisha has some options here. He could throw out the entire stew because there is simply too much contamination. He also could try to strain out the offending ingredients in the stew. The option he chooses, however, is fascinating, and it shines a light on how we might respond politically as God's people. "Get some flour," Elisha commands. When the flour has been added, Elisha begins to serve the people, "and there was nothing harmful in the pot" (2 Kings 4:41). This is a different story, to be sure, but perhaps that is precisely what makes valley stories such promising places to find political guidance.

Of course, remembering the stories of the valley also reminds us of the stories of the mountain. We can be fairly sure that something intentional is taking place in the placement of the stories in 2 Kings 3–5. In the juxtaposition, Israel is not only reminded of who they are but also of who they are not. As God's people, they must wrestle with whether they will be a people of the mountain or a people of the valley. As these narratives so quickly remind us, however, God's history is usually written in the valley.

STEPPING INTO THE KINGDOM

There are at least a few things this means for us. First, if we are going to live as people of the valley, as people who are marked, formed, and identified by stories of Yahweh's faithfulness, then we must recognize that we live in what theologians often refer to as a "time between times." The time between times refers to the idea that there are times on either side of where we are currently living, and these times help us remember and keep us hopeful. The time past reminds us of our bearings, and the time to come reminds us of where we're going as God's people.

The time we remember is the time of God's creating, found in Genesis 1 and 2. That was the time when everything was as God created it to be. There was a deep, lasting, and intimate fellowship between God and creation. In one of our favorite images from Genesis, God walks through the garden in the cool of the day (Genesis 3:8), suggesting God's nearness and the close relationship between creator and creation. That was the time when there was no death, when there was a wonderful and pervasive peace that touched every corner of creation. The whole of creation itself appears to simply be enjoying its being made so well.

The time we hope for is the time of God's re-creating. It is that time in which God will once again be all in all, and all of creation will be restored and made new. Revelation 22 paints a vivid picture of a restored Eden, complete with trees that produce fruit for the healing of the nations (Revelation 22:2). The curse levied against a rebellious creation will be lifted, and God's presence will be so fulfilling that it will light the entire city (Revelation 22:3, 5). Because Creator and creation will once again live together in right relationship, everything will be as it was intended to be.

The garden is a memory of our past. New Jerusalem is a hope for the future. We are caught between those times. We are a people of the valley. Visually, we might think of it like this:

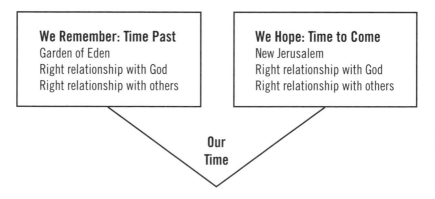

As people of the valley, we recognize that we aren't living in Eden anymore, nor are we in the New Jerusalem yet. We are a people who live *between* those times, caught between memory and hope. Eden looms large in our memories, reminding us of who we are and what we have been created for. It reminds us of where we've been. New Jerusalem stands as a beacon of hope, reminding us of where we will end up. It tells us where we're going.

For centuries, Christian theologians have been examining what it means to be a people who live in this time between times. It may mean, for instance, that we simply avoid engagement in the world. If we are simply between times, why would we want to use our time and energy engaging? Shouldn't we simply wait until the dawning of the New Jerusalem and leave the rest of the world to its own devices?

Generally, this approach is not in line with Christian theology, mainly because we believe in a God who became flesh and stepped directly into this time between the times. Simply stated, God has not abandoned this time between the times but has made a way for us to be faithful while we wait. In the incarnation of Jesus, God identified in the most tangible way with the people of the valley. God drew near to people of the valley and made God's dwelling among us, right here in this time between the times.

But in the way God redeems, God's dwelling with us was made complete when God raised Jesus from the dead and exalted him over all of creation. In the resurrection, God has overcome the most formidable power in the time between times: death. In the garden of Eden, death wasn't a factor until the fall. In the New Jerusalem, the praise of the city will be eternal and ongoing, and death will be vanquished. But in this time between those deathless times, death is a reality for us. The good news is that, in stepping into the valley, experiencing death then overcoming it in the resurrection, Jesus has overcome the most feared and potent force in this time between the times.

Christ's exaltation, too, is a gift to people in the valley. Jesus's ascension into the heavens after his resurrection is often overlooked for its incredible political and theological value. Rather than being a flashy exit, there is something significant that Christ *ascended*, being lifted up over creation. Christ's ascension sets the political reality for this time between times: Even though we have not arrived at the New Jerusalem, Christ is still Lord over creation. While we are told that a day is coming when Christ's lordship will be universally recognized (Philippians 2:9-11), Christ's ascension reminds us that his authority over creation is an objective reality in this time between times. For now, however, not everyone recognizes Christ's present authority.

If you're at all curious about what all these theological realities have to do with us now, or the way we go about living our lives, consider this: Our calling as people of the valley has everything to do with living now in the full hope of the New Jerusalem. This isn't to say we simply sit around and wish that the New Jerusalem were a reality. Rather, it means we are called to live out the political realities of the New Jerusalem, even as we live in the valley. Christian hope isn't wishful thinking about the future. Christian hope is living now in the full reality of God's future. It is living as a people who allow God's future to break into our present. It is understanding the way life goes in God's future and living that out now in the power of God's grace.

Think with us for a moment about the way life happens in the church. Every week, the body of Christ gathers to do some strange political things. We sing together. Worship of God takes priority over anything else that would divide us. We share food every time we celebrate the Lord's Supper. In many congregations, there is a time of "passing the peace" by shaking hands or sharing an embrace. At every turn, Christian worship is life lived according to the patterns of the New Jerusalem. And that begins to make our worship awfully political. It means we are arranging life, sharing resources, and forming relationships according to a particular political vision. That vision, of course, is that Christ has been exalted over creation, has overcome death, and has made a way for us to be reconciled to one another. It looks, in many ways, like life in the New Jerusalem.

This is what it means for us to live in hope of the New Jerusalem. As we allow the patterns and rhythms of life in that future city to break into our present, we become God's hopeful people of the valley. In allowing God's future to be made real in this time between times, we become the people who live with every confidence that God is writing salvation history in the valley, rather than on the mountaintop. And those people also recognize that if the valley is where God is writing the story, the valley is precisely where they want to be.

The struggle, however, is that not everyone wishes to live in the valley. In fact, many people do just about whatever they can to make their dwelling on the mountain. Living on the mountaintop means living according to the logic of the mountaintop, striving for power rather than faithfulness. In 2 Kings, we see that the mountains contain the people who live according to different stories than the stories of the valley. Rather than showcasing Yahweh's faithfulness to the meek, mountaintop life is characterized by what we see in 2 Kings 3 and 2 Kings 5: kings striving for superior power, going to war with one another, and attempting to mold the world in ways that benefit their own kingdoms. To succumb to those temptations is to fail to see that we live in a time between times.

From the vantage point of the mountaintop, kings are tempted to believe they live in *their* time, rather than Christ's time. A coronation is often a celebration of that ruler's reign, and of the hope that he or she will bring about a time of goodness and prosperity during that reign. Rarely, however, does a coronation recount the way that a peasant carpenter who associated with valley people was exalted above all creation to a place of ultimate authority. Additionally, a mountaintop approach to life rarely pauses to consider the future reality, written by God, that will come in its fullness. Rather, mountaintop life would claim that kings write their own stories and set their own agendas precisely because, when they were coronated, they proclaimed, "This is *my* time; today is *my* day." The problem is this: They forget what day it actually is.

A pastor friend of ours is fond of telling a story about a woman who loved receiving the Sunday newspaper. She looked forward to the extra content and the full-color comics. One week, her Sunday paper did not arrive. There were no color comics, no new recipe ideas, no celebrity gossip. She chalked it up to a forgetful delivery boy and went about her business. The following week, there was still no paper, and her patience began to wear thin. When yet another weekend arrived and there was no Sunday paper on her doorstep by the evening hours, she picked up the phone and called the publisher. "I'm calling to complain that my Sunday paper hasn't arrived," she told the man on the other end of the line. "Every Sunday I look forward to the comics, the crossword, and the recipe ideas, and when the paper doesn't come, I get irritated, so that's why I'm calling to complain."

There was a pause before the newspaper man spoke up. "Ma'am," he said as patiently as he could, "the reason your Sunday paper hasn't arrived yet is that today is Saturday." There was silence as the woman tried to process what she had just heard.

"I see," she replied, matter of factly. "Well, that would also explain why I was the only one at church this morning."

The consequences of not being aware what day it is can be humorous, and they can be politically problematic. We've probably seen the political rhetoric that begins to emerge when we see those who have been swayed by the temptation to believe it is *their* day. Oftentimes they mean well. They believe their particular platform will usher in a time of peace or prosperity, that their policies will truly be better than anything their political opponents can offer. We've probably also seen, then, how this rhetoric begins to set a political tone of opposition and division. One platform or party is elevated above another, and we recognize all too well the way this kind of pattern escalates. The temptation is always there to believe we are people of the mountain and that, because we are people of the mountain, we can bring about *our* time, usually by defeating the opposition.

As people of the valley, however, we recognize that we live in the time between times. We live in memory of Eden and in hope of the New Jerusalem, but we also acknowledge that in his ascension,

Christ has been given ultimate authority over all of creation. Even in this time between times, today is still God's time. The mistake of a mountaintop approach to political life is the failure to acknowledge that even today is God's day.

In declaring that this is *their* day, mountaintop kings assume that their authority is ultimate. They assume that their agendas and plans do not need to be submitted to any authority higher than their own. But if we have seen the story of God's salvation clearly, we must contest such an approach and instead confess that the authority given to earthly kings is one that falls under Christ's lordship. Those who are placed in positions of authority, then, do not rule according to *their* day but according to God's. In other words, they have been given provisional, but not ultimate, authority. When rulers are tempted to think they are governing according to *their* time, when they begin to trust that their policies or platform will bring about peace, even at the expense of the opposition, they fail to realize that they are living in a time between the times when God will establish ultimate peace, and they begin to become those who are tempted to imitate God.

Theologian Karl Barth was particularly aware of this temptation, especially as he reflected on Paul's letter to the Roman Christians. "Must not the existing order, the order that has already been found, seem the very incarnation of triumphant unrighteousness to the man who is seeking after God and His Order? … Rulers! What are rulers but men? What are they but men hypocritically engaged in setting things in order, in order that they may…ensure themselves securely against the riddle of their own existence?"[14] Barth's rhetoric is strong, but the principle is clear: Political rulers are not intended to be in a position of ultimate authority. At its best, political rule is the work that must be done to maintain a provisional peace in the time between the peace of Eden and the peace of the New Jerusalem.

---

14. Karl Barth, *The Epistle to the Romans* (Oxford: Oxford University Press, 1968), 478.

Political rule, then, does not serve the agenda of the ruler, nor does it impart permission upon the ruler to craft the agenda of his or her choosing. Rather, political rule done well recognizes that it is neither ultimate nor eternal.

Fourth-century philosopher and theologian Augustine of Hippo devoted substantial amounts of writing to this idea. True peace, he argued, is that which is ordered under God's reign, and that political rule is a service enacted rightly under God's authority, for the sake of establishing peace as best we can until God is once again all in all.[15] Political rulers are called to do the best they can, Augustine taught, and to establish peace as appointed representatives of God, so to speak, who is the one who can and will bring true and ultimate peace. When rulers begin to rule in such a way that serves their self-created agendas, however, things begin to go awry. When rulers fail to realize that they are temporary fill-ins, when they fail to realize that they are governing in the time between times, their perspective becomes skewed, and the door is opened to the inevitable clash of opposing political philosophies.

In the same way that political rulers are called to remember what day it is, so too are people of the valley. In many ways, when people of the valley acknowledge that they live in a time between times, they have an accurate knowledge of what day it is. They know that today is a day for waiting but that it is not yet the day when God is all in all. People of the valley understand both that the day of Christ's return will be a day for rejoicing and worshiping because God will be all in all, and that that great day of rejoicing has not yet arrived.

Part of what 2 Kings attempts to communicate is that kings often forget what day it is. Sometimes this means that the king recognizes that the day is coming when God will reign, but by virtue of being human, kings often convince themselves that they can somehow

---

15. Saint Augustine, Bishop of Hippo, *The City of God against the Pagans*, R. W. Dyson, ed. (Cambridge: Cambridge University Press, 1998), 909-64.

bring that day about, even before it has actually arrived. Kings aren't the only ones who sometimes flirt with this temptation, however. The church's history in North America is peppered with attempts to usher in the kingdom of God through the effort of the people, through enacting certain legislation, or simply by advocating enough political reform that we can bring about what we pray for, that God's will would be done on earth as it is in heaven. This is not to say that Christians shouldn't engage politically in such a way that reflects the coming kingdom of God. The point is that we must remember it is not our kingdom at all, but God's. When God's kingdom comes in its fullness, we must remember that it will be God's day, not ours. As well-meaning as we may be, the day is not ours to claim. Our calling is to faithfully live out the reality of the coming kingdom in the midst of the present one, a reality made possible by virtue of Christ's resurrection and exaltation.

If we are honest about what we see around us politically, especially in the church, it is people of the valley who often look to the mountains, see a ruler or a party or a platform, and then try to climb out of the valley to the top of that mountain. The temptation is strong because the rulers or political parties are so convinced that they have the right way of governing, that the day of fulfillment has arrived, and that they just need to beat their detractors back so we can all see how great *their* day will be. They are deeply convinced that their policies are so good that if their opponents would get out of the way, everything would be fantastic. That kind of certainty begins to attract the attention of valley people. The rhetoric from the mountaintop can be so loud, so brash, and so self-confident that we can sometimes be tempted to begin to climb out of the valley and align ourselves with life on the mountaintop.

The trouble with doing so is that life on the mountain is different. There are different stories told, and a different set of things are valued and seen as good. On the mountain, kings write the story of history, often by winning in a battle over a threatening opponent. On the mountain, a common comment you may hear would go something like: "We'd all be better off if we could just vote the (fill in the name of a political party here) out of office so our people could be in office. That's when everything will get better." The troubling idea here is that putting our party into office, whatever that party may be, is an attempt to bring God's day about on our own. We should also add here that we've already seen what tends to happen in the history that kings on mountains are writing. Keep in mind that 2 Kings 3 paints a clear picture of warring kings going home no better off than they started.

In the valley—Yahweh's valley, remember—the stories told are of God's faithfulness to the meek and the humble and quiet ways that God brings about salvation. In the valley, history is not advanced simply by eliminating the enemy but by God's faithfulness to the people who live there and who are formed by the stories of the valley. In the valley the comments that we share with one another point to the faithfulness of God, no matter who happens to be the majority party in office. People of the valley wait in hope for God's day to arrive, but they know that when God's day comes, it will be God's doing and we will have all the more reason to rejoice. As people of the valley, we realize it is not the kings on the mountains who write our story; it is the faithfulness of Yahweh, a faithfulness that often comes to us in ways that don't appear powerful on the surface.

Sometimes, when we fall to the temptation to think that our rulers, our policies, or even our own political parties can somehow establish ultimate peace and goodness (if everyone would just get on board and do it our way), we forget what day it is. We forget that today is not the day when ultimate authority has been established. Therefore, as people of the valley, we are called to remember what day it is. We remember that it is a day between the times when God's authority is realized in its fullness. We remember that it is not yet the day when God will set all things right and will once again be fully recognized as the ultimate authority. But this also means that we realize it's also not the day when any one particular political party, ruler, or platform is all in all. We recognize not only that human political rulers occupy their offices under the authority of the Creator but also that their platforms are not capable of ushering in the complete fullness of the New Jerusalem. People of the valley realize that they occupy a time between times, that no human ruler will be the one who can establish a true and lasting peace. It's their perspective as people of the valley, formed by the stories of God's faithfulness to the weak and cast-aside, that allows them to see this different political reality, and to realize that they do not need to climb the mountain but can remain in the valley.

But waiting isn't the only thing people of the valley can do. A large part of what it means to be people of the valley is actually twofold: We wait, but we also engage. We wait because we recognize that God is the ultimate authority, and that when kings, rulers, or other leaders make claims of ultimacy, they are mistaken. We wait because we have hope in what God is bringing. But remember, Christian hope is not wishful thinking. It's living into the coming reality. It is living the reality of what's still coming in the midst of what's happening now. Therefore, hope calls us to engage. If hope really is living out a future reality in the midst of a present one, we can't express hope if we aren't engaging our present reality with the hope of God's future. As people of the valley, we are people who do not withdraw from the present reality but engage it in hope with the enduring belief that what we are living out in the present age is not our attempt to bring God's kingdom but to live in faithful accordance to the one who has been faithful to us in the valley.

We are not called to be whisked out of the world. We are called to engage as people of hope, precisely because we know what kind of future God is bringing, and we seek to live as people of that future even before it's made fully present. This is why as pastors we encourage our people to engage in political life rather than dismiss it. But we do so with the encouragement that they vote as people of the valley, rather than as people attempting to climb to a particular mountaintop. We want our people to engage, to vote, to protest, to campaign, to invest, and to sacrifice but always and only for the sake of being a people attempting to live out the rhythms of the New Jerusalem in the here and now. In the world of kings, engagement serves to advance the prospects of one party or candidate, but in the world of the kingdom, the engagement of a valley people is always for the sake of allowing God's future to break into the present. We want our people to engage, but with the knowledge that we seek God's kingdom, rather than the kingdom of any given political figure or party. When people of the valley engage in the political life of their society, it is never to empower a king on a mountaintop but to say to the world, "Our God is faithful, and this is what it looks like when we live out that faithfulness."

That kind of engagement will rarely make sense to kings and those who occupy the mountaintops. Sometimes it will mean that party lines are less important to us than they once were. Sometimes it will mean we support causes championed by different political parties. But it will always mean our engagement will be a faithful witness to the God who has been faithful to us in the valley.

In speaking of engagement, let's return to the story of Elisha and the pot of stew. As you'll recall, when Elisha's companions declare that there is death in the pot, Elisha orders that flour be added to the stew, and the noxious concoction immediately becomes a palatable meal. Bible scholars are not in complete agreement on what this signifies. It could simply be a sign of prophetic power. But, since this story is tucked among the other valley stories of 2 Kings 4, we think it suggests something about what it means to be people of the valley.

Again, Elisha could throw everything out because it is too contaminated, and this is definitely a certain kind of political temptation for us. As we preached through 2 Kings, a couple came to visit our church for the first time the week Shawna preached on the story of Elisha and the deadly stew. The husband in this visiting couple was a decorated and successful military officer in the United States

Marines, ascending to the rank of general before his retirement. On their way out of church that day, he had tears in his eyes. "You have to believe me when I say this," he said. "If this next election doesn't go my way, I have every intention of moving out of the country. I've just had it. It's too corrupt." In essence, this man was prepared to throw out the whole stew. There was too much death in the pot for his liking, and he was ready to give it all up. The temptation to throw the whole thing out because of a given offensive element is a strong one for people of the valley, but it ought to be resisted.

Elisha also has the option of trying to strain out everything that is harmful in the pot. The problem with this option is that everything's already cooked together. It would be next to impossible to separate out the life-giving from the harmful, much in the same way that even a little corruption works its way through large sectors of a society fairly quickly. If we are honest with ourselves, we can probably recognize that corruption has touched us in a lot of ways, simply by virtue of the fact that we are interconnected people. Every time we buy something, for example, we join ourselves to a vast network of connections, some of which are unjust and harmful. In a globalized world, ethicists and theologians are finding a whole new set of questions about the ways in which we perpetuate harm to one another, even unknowingly or unwillingly.

Politically, attempting to strain out harmful ingredients is a fairly prominent temptation. If we could just un-elect all those who have brought corruption into the offices of political power, we'd be on the right track, goes this line of reasoning. We are still unsure, however, about which would be more difficult: straining out the noxious presence of a plant that has already been cooked into a stew, or removing corrupt leaders from their positions in an effort to cleanse our political system. You may see that the likelihood of either task succeeding is fairly slim, yet we are often drawn to this strategy, probably because it's a story that comes to us so loudly from the mountaintops.

There is a lot around us that's harmful and bitter and not life-giving, and we can spend a lot of time and energy trying to strain out all the harmful things in our society. But as we look at this particular story that shapes us to be people of the valley, we see Elisha bypassing the option of straining out the death in the pot, and working instead to simply add in life. This is precisely why we encourage engagement, even as we wait for God to be all in all. We encourage engagement in the systems and cultures of our day not because we need to work hard to eliminate what's harmful. Instead, this story shows us that, as people of the valley, we just need to add in a lot more good.

As people of the valley, we are not called to escape the world, or to throw it all away; we are called to engage, and we are called to be poured out into the midst of a broken world. As people of the valley, we are those who have been formed by the stories of God's faithfulness, and throughout much of Scripture, God's salvation rarely looks like God coming to eradicate the bad, but it often looks like God pouring in lots of good, until goodness overcomes that which leads to death.

The mentality of the kings on the mountain is to strain out what they see as bad; to take those who oppose them and get rid of them. For those of us who live in a political system dominated by two parties, this is often the story that calls to us from the mountaintop. We tend to be a people who choose one party then try to weed the bad out of our political system by getting our party people elected. As people of the valley, though, we are not called to begin the work of straining out the bad but to become the good that is poured into broken, harmful, and oppressive systems and cultures.

Even more astounding is that the history of God's salvation has included God calling a people out to be the good that is poured into a world marred with death and corruption. But God's faithfulness most potently includes God's own self being poured out into creation for the sake of overcoming the harmful things that have mixed death into the pot. And as people of Yahweh's valley, we look to the stories of the presence of Yahweh—Emmanuel—with us, being poured out, so that whatever has been causing death is rendered inert, and we can feast once again, knowing there is no longer death in the pot.

THE RECOUNT

The World of Kings:	The World of the Kingdom:
Believes the story is written by kings on mountaintops	Believes the story is written by God's faithfulness to people in the valley
Is tempted to think that ultimate authority is awarded to the most powerful ruler	Confesses that ultimate authority is God's
Often considers that the day belongs to the most powerful king	Acknowledges that this day is a time between times when God's authority is not fully seen by all
Is marked by living out the ruler's agendas, even at great cost to any opponents	Is marked by living out God's future in the present situation
Acts on its own agendas and plans, waiting only for opportunity	Waits for God's day to come fully but engages in the meantime, acting according to God's reign
Desires to live on the mountaintop so that one's particular party or faction can be in control	Is content to live in the valley, receiving the bounty of God's faithfulness

PURCHASING POWER AND THE POWER TO PURCHASE

2 KINGS 5:1-19

We always love to learn a new turn of phrase. Clever arrangements of words and ideas are fun for us. Part of what we do as pastors requires us to work in the medium of language, so we have come to love the art of wordcraft. When it comes to describing the scene that unfolds in 2 Kings 5, a particularly favored phrase of ours is *decorated irrelevance*. We wish we had coined it, but it actually comes from Walter Brueggemann, who has used this phrase accurately to describe what's happening as the king of Aram sends his top commander to Israel, hoping he can be healed of the disease that eats away at his body.

STEPPING INTO THE STORY

Naaman, the commander of Aram's army, is described as an impressive warrior who has been able to deliver multiple victories for his king and country. In the narrative of 2 Kings 5, we get an immediate sense of just how important he is in Aram. The first couple verses in chapter 5 tell us not only about his importance but also that he has been a champion for Aram. Naaman is remembered for his prowess as a warrior, and his expertise as a soldier is celebrated by his king. The writer of 2 Kings gives God the credit for Naaman's victories, but that probably isn't the case for the Aramean king. In the king's eyes, Naaman is the one to be celebrated, not God. Even though 2 Kings credits God, Naaman is an outsider to Israel. He is a Gentile. He is an Aramean.

If you remember, Aram is one of Israel's favorite sparring partners; it seems that throughout the narrative of 2 Kings, Israel and Aram are always going to war over something. In the grand scheme of things, though, neither Israel nor Aram is all that politically important in the ancient near east. In the long-cast shadows of towering countries like Egypt and Babylon, nations like Aram and Israel are somewhat inconsequential, so it becomes fairly easy for Israel and Aram to fight each other rather than risk absolute destruction by going to war with a superpower. Naaman, then, is the great champion of Israel's political nemesis, the nation with which Israel is always feuding. If, as we see in 5:1, God has given Aram victories against their political rivals through Naaman, it is reasonable to assume that Israel has been on the losing end of many of those victories. It would be accurate, then, to say that Naaman is an enemy of Israel. Yet we are told in no uncertain terms that the God of Israel has given Naaman victories, so we are left to consider just how God would use this enemy of Israel for their benefit.

When Naaman is stricken with leprosy, however, the king of Aram knows he is at risk of losing one of his most valuable warriors. On a tip from an Israelite girl who has been taken into Aramean slavery, the king of Aram decides to appeal to the king of Israel. Right away we begin to see that something is amiss: The Israelite girl recommended that Naaman see a prophet of God who is living in Israel, and the king of Aram decides instead to appeal to the king of Israel.

We shouldn't miss the irony of what's happening here. First, we see a young girl who has been taken into slavery by Aramean warriors suggesting a course of action to try to save the life of the greatest of all the Aramean warriors. In and of itself, this attracts our attention and gives us pause to consider why she wants to save someone who belongs to the people who have taken her into slavery. But the larger issue arises as we see the way the Aramean king responds to her suggestion. A slave girl with no power to speak of suggests that Naaman appeal to a prophet of Israel. In response, the king opts to send his most powerful warrior to the *king* of Israel. In some sense, this is like hearing the weather forecaster suggest warm clothes for the day and immediately rushing to find your favorite shorts and t-shirt. "Thank you for the advice. I think I'll do the exact opposite."

The message we should receive yet again, however, is not simply that the king doesn't seem to be listening very closely so much as that he can't seem to conceive of a reality in which a powerless slave girl (whose powerlessness is confirmed by the absence of her name) could offer him anything that would effect real change. In the king's mind, if you want something, there is a way to get it, and that way isn't listening to powerless slave girls. The girl offers a way toward healing, and he can't see it. In a complete distortion of her recommendation, he seeks out the highest power *he* knows—the completely wrong person in Israel. When you live in the world of kings, you often have trouble seeing value in the world of the kingdom. Rather than going to the prophet of God, who can actually do something for Naaman, he goes to the king of Israel, who can only tear his clothes and wonder if this is some kind of political trap being set by the king of Aram. Once again, the writer of 2 Kings is attempting to show us that kings will do what kings do.

This is where the phrase we like so much applies to the story of 2 Kings 5. As the king's envoy departs Aram for Israel, Naaman is not only in possession of a letter from one king to another but also enough money to buy a palace. There is pomp, there is gold, there is a display of power—and none of it matters because it's going to the wrong place. All of it is *decorated irrelevance*. It's like a cat in a tuxedo. It's fun to look at, but it's not getting anything done. As a people, we often get caught up in the decorated irrelevance of political life.

As the story unfolds, Naaman eventually finds his way to Elisha's house with all his servants and his silver and his gold. Consider the contrast of what that must look like. Naaman's impressive entourage comes to rest outside the humble, plain home of a prophet. And on top of that, Elisha doesn't even come out of his house to see Naaman. We can probably understand Naaman's rage at this insult. With all his signs of importance, with the circus of significance he has brought with him, he expects an equal reception, but Elisha only sends out a servant with instructions for Naaman to wash himself in the Jordan River.

Consider Naaman's position. Ensconced in a spectacle of horses, chariots, and the trappings of importance, he has not gone into Israel unnoticed. He hasn't slipped into the city under cover of darkness but in the back of a thundering chariot—why? Because he has leprosy. That probably hasn't escaped the attention of the people who came out of their houses to see what all the fuss is about. Has all of this been one large ruse designed to humiliate the great warrior champion of Israel's political nemesis? Has he been tricked into parading himself through the streets to allow his enemies to see the effects of his illness? Is that what this is all about? If that question is present in Naaman's mind, we shouldn't be surprised that he becomes as angry as he does.

Still, Elisha has told Naaman exactly what he needs to do to be cleansed of his disease. Elisha hasn't held back what Naaman came for, so why is Naaman upset? Perhaps it is because Elisha does not meet Naaman's spectacle in kind. Elisha doesn't join in the parade or take part in the hoopla. He doesn't really try to sell Naaman on a plan to cure his leprosy. It's like the difference between buying a car from a showroom and buying from Craigslist. In the showroom, there are bright lights and a freshly waxed exterior and a salesperson in a fancy suit, and even though you know nothing of the car itself, it looks really nice and you feel good about buying that car. On Craigslist, it's a website with a cell-phone picture of a car in a dimly lit garage. It might be the greatest car in the world, but you sure don't feel all that good about making the purchase. And if you do show up to test drive the car, it's probably not going to be waiting in a room with fancy lights and a sales expert in a nice suit. It's most likely going to be a regular guy with a car in a parking lot.

Naaman came looking for the showroom treatment and gets a parking lot. We like to be sold on things. We like for there to be a bit of spectacle that comes with the purchase because it makes us feel good about what we've just bought. Naaman doesn't get a spectacle. Elisha sees all of Naaman's pageantry it for what it is: decorated irrelevance. It isn't that Elisha wants to hold back the blessing of grace from Naaman; it's more that he's attempting to signal that grace doesn't require a parade or a show. It doesn't even require all the silver and gold that Naaman has brought with him. Grace can't be bought in the same way that political favor can because grace isn't a commodity that comes with a price tag.

Begrudgingly, Naaman finally goes to the Jordan River and follows Elisha's instructions for washing himself there, and just as Elisha said, he is made clean. Here, Naaman has received the free grace of God, and still he doesn't know what to do with that reality, so he returns to Elisha to attempt to pay him for his services. The prophet's answer, however, is decisive: "As surely as the LORD lives, whom I serve, I will not accept a thing" (2 Kings 5:16). Elisha recognizes that nothing is owed to him because he hasn't provided Naaman anything that isn't a free gift from God.

STEPPING INTO THE KINGDOM

When we encounter this story, we can see that there are quite a few things that distinguish the world of kings from the world of the kingdom. First, we can't help but notice who gets noticed. The Aramean king will listen to the slave girl but only to a point. Very quickly, his embeddedness in the world of kings overcomes his ability to hear what the girl has to say, so that, when he does send Naaman to Israel, he sends him to the wrong person.

As we walk through more of 2 Kings, we'll continue to see that those who live in the world of kings are rarely able to hear powerless people speaking. Even when a message of hope and healing is on their lips, 2 Kings illuminates the way in which world-of-kings people have trouble listening to those who do not hold a position of power in that world. This won't be the last instance in 2 Kings that we'll see a king who can't quite seem to hear a powerless person speaking, so it is to our benefit to begin hearing what 2 Kings has to say to us on this issue.

If the world of kings is characterized by people rarely listening to the voices of the powerless, it is reasonable to assume that things are different in the world of the kingdom. In the world of the kingdom, the voice of the powerless is the one that often delivers good news. But prophets and the powerless are rarely given ear by kings and warriors in this story, leaving us to hear the story, distinguish between the worlds, and be challenged as to which world will be our political home.

Might the citizens of the world of the kingdom find a way to give a voice to the powerless? What kind of politics might emerge as a result? Could it be that the strange, subversive history of God's salvation story advances upon the words of those who have little or no power in the world of kings? What might happen to us if we were to listen to them, to give them audience, and to value them as a king values his most powerful warrior? Again, the world of the kingdom functions in an upside-down way, but that's exactly how God's story of salvation gets told.

Another motif in 2 Kings 5 is that kings tend to impress one another to gain favors or advantages. They send their most powerful warriors and lots of money, but at the end of the day, appealing to a king when you need a prophet won't get you anywhere. Still, the

Aramean king can only see this one way of making something happen. Even when he has a person standing near to him, giving him the advice that would give him what he needs, he can't see that advice as a legitimate course of action because appealing to prophets is not what kings do.

Prophets are problematic politically. Their miracles often seem to come with a demand for some kind of change. They turn things upside down, which is difficult for people at the top. Perhaps this is why the king of Aram decides to appeal to a king rather than a prophet. Kings can deal nicely with other kings, but prophets are problematic and messy. But the king of Israel can't deliver what the king of Aram needs, and that is a large part of what the writer of 2 Kings is attempting to communicate. When you go to a king instead of a prophet for healing and wholeness, even if you appeal to the king on kingly terms, it's all going to end up being decorated irrelevance.

This concept reminds us a lot of what we see happen in the news media during elections, especially in cable news. Election night coverage is filled with all kinds of spectacle, and little of it makes any difference. During the 2008 presidential election, CNN debuted their new hologram technology, allowing a reporter to appear to be standing in the studio with the anchor, even though she was hundreds of miles away. It was touted as groundbreaking. It was something no one had ever seen on live television before. And none of it mattered for actually providing coverage of the election. It certainly did not do anything to shift the outcome of the election altogether. It was just one piece of technology used that night that created a bit of noise but wasn't altogether substantive. It was decorated irrelevance.

While money and spectacle carry a lot of weight in the dealings of kings, it really isn't seen as the currency of the kingdom of God. The economy of God's kingdom is one that operates on the freedom of exchange, on the superabundant plentitude of grace. But as we have seen, grace makes little sense in the world of kings. The world of kings operates on the basis of price tags, and you can't put a price tag on grace.

Shawna's first staff ministry assignment was at a United Methodist church on the outskirts of Chicago. Part of her assignment was to teach a confirmation class to eighth graders in the church. For churches who baptize their children as infants, confirmation is an opportunity for the children to take hold of their baptism in a cognitive way, and allow the church to invite the Spirit to confirm the grace that was present at their baptism as infants. The classes leading up to confirmation, then, had everything to do with the students owning their faith, and being conversant in what it was to be a follower of Christ.

Full of excitement and energy to bestow upon those kids the good things of God, Shawna came to the first class ready to talk with them about the deep things of God, to introduce them to the beautiful mystery of the Christian faith, and to wrestle with their questions of ultimate concern—questions about life and death and resurrection. But those questions seemed far away from the minds of that group. Instead, they asked, "How many of these classes do I need to attend to still be confirmed?" "Do I *have* to go to church on Sundays *and* to youth group on Wednesday nights to be confirmed?" "Can my boy scout trips count toward my required community service for confirmation?" While the practice of confirmation was about accepting the astounding gift of God's grace, the students approached it with the shrewd calculus of attempting to decipher the bare minimum of what it would cost them to get what they wanted. Shawna had prepared to orient them to the mystery and beauty of the Christian faith, to help them get caught up in the amazing realities of God's grace, but the students couldn't see any of that because they were only looking at the price tag.

But again, you can't buy grace. As the class wore on, a moment of blunt honesty caught Shawna, who asked the students, "Why are you here? Why do you want to do this?" Most of them gave apathetic answers about fulfilling parental expectations. "If that's the case," Shawna told them, "I don't have to confirm you. This church doesn't have to confirm you. If you are not here to confirm your faith in Christ, if all you're here to do is fulfill the minimum requirements and go through a ceremony, we will not confirm you." The students looked back at her with a bit of fear in their eyes, not only because an adult was getting real with them, but because in that moment, Shawna had ripped the price tag away from the grace of confirmation, and suddenly, they didn't know what it was worth anymore. They didn't know what they had to do or what was expected of them, so now they were lost.

We probably like price tags more than we care to admit. They let us know how much things cost, how much things are worth, and how much we need to sacrifice to obtain the items we want. Certainly, our political system operates according to price tags. In the 2012 presidential election cycle, the campaigns of the major candidates reported spending a combined $2 billion, breaking records for the amount of money spent on an election. This figure did not include many anonymous donations, filtered through political action committees, nor did it count the amount of money spent from other outside groups not directly affiliated with one candidate or the other. Of course, the amount of money spent on an election doesn't necessarily guarantee the outcome; in 2012 the biggest spenders weren't necessarily the winners in all congressional and local campaigns. You can't buy an election simply by spending more money than the opponent, but you certainly can't win an election for free either. Most of us know that there were more than two names on the presidential ballot, but few of us could probably remember what those names were, primarily because those candidates did not have access to the same financial resources as the candidates whose names we do remember. With that reality staring us in the face, it feels an awful lot like elections come down to price tags, and perhaps this shouldn't surprise us, since this has been the way the world of kings has operated for a long, long time.

Price tags are what Naaman wants to know about. "How much gold do I need to bring to get what I want? How much silver?" he might have asked. "To whom do I have to go? Whom do I have to impress? Doesn't everything have a price tag?" This is how Naaman lives, so when he is offered free grace, he doesn't know what to do with it. In fact, even when what he has come looking for is offered to him, he almost walks away from it because he doesn't know what to do with something that comes without a price tag. And Elisha rips the price tag away from grace when he extends it to Naaman freely.

What might it be like if serving God weren't about price tags? What would it be like if gathering with others for worship weren't about price tags? How would that change things? How might our churches be transformed if all those who call themselves Christians understood how free God's grace truly is?

In North America, many churches experience an interesting phenomenon around Christmas and Easter. Many people who are loosely affiliated with the church return for at least one service, whether that is to fulfill a cultural or family obligation, or perhaps because those who show up for a service or two here and there look at grace and see a price tag. They calculate what the bare minimum is to relate to God, and to receive grace. After all, you wouldn't want to pay more for something than you need to, right?

As pastors, we often look around our congregation and are struck by those who clearly haven't attached a price tag to grace. They are the ones who aren't at all interested in the bare minimum. Rather, they are the ones who are at church more than we are. They are the ones who give themselves fully to their devotion, and they are like this because they have understood how freely grace has been given to them.

A young man named Josh in our church is a good example. He came up through the youth ministry, has now entered young adulthood, and is more passionate about his commitment to the church than ever. When he has transportation to get him to church, he'll use it, but there are many weeks we see Josh setting out on foot for home after staying late to lock up the building or attending a meeting after the service. He regularly gives his weeknights to help in the youth ministry or children's ministry, even after a long day at work. While many others his age might be counting the cost, while they might spend time considering the lowest bar they need to clear, Josh hasn't really considered his commitment to be something that fulfills a minimum but is, rather, a response to God's free grace.

When we work with people in a pastoral context, we often find that those who are willing to give everything are those who never had their eye on the price tag but were the grateful and willing recipients of free, unbounded grace. When serving God is about more than the bare minimum, when it is simply the grateful response to free grace, the cost is of no consequence.

There's something else we ought to see about grace in 2 Kings 5, though, and that is the way God continues to use outsiders as conduits of God's grace. Naaman is an outsider, as Jesus reminds us in Luke 4:27, yet we see that God's grace isn't cut off by his outsiderness. A slave girl from Israel is an outsider in Aram, but God uses her in an unexpected way to bestow grace upon Naaman. If there's anything we can see in the stories of 2 Kings, it is that God uses unexpected people in unexpected places to bestow unexpected grace.

As the votes were counted and precincts reported in November 2012, many people in our own congregation felt that their guy had won. Others felt that their guy lost, and that caused some pain. That pain too often turns to bitterness, which turns to disillusionment or slander, and when faced with that kind of temptation, we probably need to ask ourselves, *Is there anyone who is outside the scope of God's grace? Is there any event through which God cannot work?* For those who feel as if their candidate lost, the challenge of 2 Kings 5 is probably something along these lines: Is God's grace so bounded that God can't use someone from a different political party to be a means of God's grace? Could it be that God could even use the guy you voted against to govern with wisdom, or is God's grace reserved only for those with whom we agree? God has long used unexpected people, even those who did not seek to follow God. Would we be willing to look for the grace-filled ways God may be using a political leader we didn't vote for, or will we stop looking for grace and instead allow the pain of loss to turn into the bitterness of disillusionment?

To those who felt as if their guy won, 2 Kings 5 speaks in a different way: Remember that the world of kings cannot heal us. Remember that it cannot be our true salvation. Remember that the king of Israel is right to tear his robes when he is asked to heal Naaman, and that his response is equally true: "Am I God? Can I kill and bring back to life?" Even if our candidate wins the election, we must remember that no amount of political power can bring the kind of healing that Naaman seeks, nor the kind of healing for which our world groans. Not all of the gold or silver, not the largest entourage, nor the greatest number of attack drones and fighter aircraft can heal what's broken about our world. Only the grace of God can do that.

A host of theologians have attempted to point out that the world of kings cannot be our salvation, though it is often the case that even the most cogent argument cannot convince us of this nearly as effectively as the collision of worlds when God's grace is offered freely in a price-tag world. Still, the way theologians have helped us on this issue should not be overlooked. One of our favorite approaches has been offered by William Cavanaugh, a theologian who has lived under one of the most oppressive totalitarian regimes in modern political history. Cavanaugh traces the philosophical history of Western political theory, demonstrating that those theorists who have been most influential (John Locke, David Hume, Jean-Jacques Rousseau, and Thomas Hobbes, among others) all share a commitment to a type of modern individualism that requires a contract theory to explain how human beings can work together as a society.[16] That is, each of the influential political philosophers understood humans as completely autonomous individuals first, linked only loosely by the idea that we must be fair to one another, usually by making contracts with one another. As they understood it, humans were not closely knit creatures of relationality but those for whom violence against one another is only a few short steps away, making contracts (such as governmental constitutions) necessary to maintain the rights of these unrelated individuals.

As Cavanaugh argues, this has led our political imagination to be shaped by contract theory, or the idea that the way we can relate to one another is only by making contracts with one another because we cannot be trusted to relate to one another outside of implicit or explicit agreements not to harm one another. To cast this in the terms we have been using in this chapter, we might say that just as Naaman's political vision has been so deeply formed by presenting silver and gold to get what he wants, our political vision has been equally shaped by the contract theory that comes with an understanding of humans as total and complete individuals, not needing one another to be who they are. In other words, since we can't *really* trust one another, since we aren't *really* related to one another, we need to make sure that the person on the other end of the relationship isn't taking advantage of us, so a contract or agreement must be the basis of our relationship. If contracts and agreements are the only way we can relate to one another in a political sense, price tags have won the day. Contracts tell us exactly what we get and exactly what it will cost us.

If contracts and price tags are the primary basis for human relationship, it shouldn't surprise us that the violence of our world is as pervasive as it is. If we are led to believe we are not truly related in some deep sense to the one we are about to harm, it removes a barrier

---

16. William T. Cavanaugh, *Theopolitical Imagination: Christian Practices of Space and Time* (London and New York: T&T Clark, 2002).

of empathic suspension, the sense that we should stop for a moment and consider how our actions might harm others. The events leading up to the financial crisis of 2008 are but one example of the way in which a political vision of contract-based life allows for action that we might even classify as violent. As financial managers began to package and repackage mortgages, slicing them up into new commodities to be bought and sold, some began to raise concern that such practices would initiate a cataclysmic financial downturn, affecting the well-being of tens of millions of people. As millions of insecure subprime mortgages were offered to potential homeowners, those same mortgages were bundled into securities that were bought and sold by large banks and financial institutions at an incredible profit. At the time, however, there was nothing overtly illegal about such transactions, nor did the millions of contracts undergirding the mortgages prohibit this kind of behavior.

Bankers and financiers opted to see the world in the political terms we have outlined above: Persons are fundamentally individuals, unrelated to one another; therefore, if one person enters into a bad business deal, the consequences stay with that individual. The problem arose when this approach ignored the fundamental political reality that we are much more related to one another than we realized. As homeowners began to default on mortgages they could not afford, the interconnectivity made it impossible for mortgage companies and banks to untangle the web of millions of points of overlap and connection; the whole world began to feel the effects of how deeply connected we are to one another.

If we can accept that we really are truly as individualized as Hobbes, Locke, and others would have us believe, the political world of price tags makes a lot of good sense. If we really are fundamentally disconnected from one another, contracts make plenty of political sense. We would simply be free to go about making whatever kind of deals we want to make, so long as those deals did not violate the contracts we have with other individuals, or encroach upon the rights of other individuals. But what happens when the reality of our related-ness comes into a sobering collision with our political assumption that we are total and complete individuals? What do you do with the reality that a deal we made has lasting consequences, not just for us, but for hundreds of other people down the line?

While there are a host of issues that can be uncovered in questions like these, what we want to suggest is that some of the deepest hurts of our time, the most profound political problems, stem from the flawed notion that our actions will not have consequences on others because we are individuals and that our business stays with us. So long as our political vision isolates us from our neighbors, we are essentially free to commit any act so long as that act does not encroach upon the legal rights of our neighbor, even if we know that our action might be detrimental to our neighbor in some way. Perhaps we pass another law or write another contract, meant to prevent such transgressions. But there will never be enough laws, and there will never be enough contracts to address the root cause of why we would be willing to do something harmful to someone else in the first place. There will never be enough laws to heal our deepest pain as a society.

This is why Cavanaugh suggests that the practice of celebrating the Lord's Supper is one of the ways Christians practice a "counter-politic" that is not based on price tags or contracted exchanges but on free grace. As Christians gather around Christ's table and are invited to partake of his broken body and spilled blood, there is also an invitation to participate in the free grace of God that characterizes the very essence of Christ's coming, life, death, and resurrection. Communion, then, is far more than eating bread and drinking wine; it is participation in the grace that God pours out on creation. Participation in God's grace is what Cavanaugh describes as "a threat to the formal mechanism of contract, which assumes that we are *essentially* individuals who enter into relationship with one another only when it is to one's individual advantage to do so."[17] The reality that the grace offered to us in Christ is utterly and completely free runs counter to the idea that we humans can only be related to one another in contractual terms. Rather, we can be related to one another in and through the free grace that God has offered in Jesus Christ. We can begin to envision and imagine others as those to whom we are truly related, rather than those to whom we are contractually obligated.

As long as we continue to occupy a political world based on price tags and contracts, as long as we continue to see one another as radical individuals who are not related to one another except for the contracts into which we enter, we must rely on a system of governance whose main task is to ensure that the rights of one individual are not transgressed by another. Often, that means that the state's task is to maintain space between individuals, to be sure that they don't encroach upon one another in a violation of individual rights. Again, however, we need to begin to wrestle with the fact that the Christian faith has never seen its purpose as to maintain individual rights but to prayerfully live into the reality of God's kingdom coming "on earth as it is in heaven," which has at least something to do with the biblical notion of reconciliation. Whereas the state's function is to maintain separation between individuals, the kingdom functions by bringing people together in reconciled relationship.

In both Romans 5 and 2 Corinthians 5, the apostle Paul makes explicit the connection between God's reconciliation to humans as the foundation for humans being reconciled to one another. "All this is from God," Paul tells us, "who reconciled us to himself through Christ and gave us the ministry of reconciliation" (2 Corinthians 5:18). According to Paul, the free grace of being reconciled to God in Christ is simultaneously a call to enter the ministry of reconciliation. As God's salvation is made full among humans, it includes being

---

17. Cavanaugh, *Theopolitical Imagination*, 44.

reconciled to one another and the healing of our relationships with and among one another.

As we have seen in 2 Kings 5, the king does not have the power to heal what is truly, deeply wrong with us, and as we explore the notion of free grace in a price-tag political world, we are also beginning to see that kings and political mechanisms can perhaps take us to the point of maintaining individual rights, but they are not equipped to take us beyond rights to the point of reconciliation. So long as our political imagination operates exclusively in the mode of contracts and price tags, it cannot bring the healing of relational reconciliation "on earth as it is in heaven." Indeed, reconciliation is the benefit of God's grace given and freely received.

So long as the world of kings operates according to the notion that favor can be bought and sold, and that political power is inextricably intertwined with purchasing power, it will not be able to come to terms with the reality of grace freely given. While Naaman's political vision is deeply formed by the world of kings, rather than the world of the kingdom, we must admit that his vision is an accurate representation of the world of kings. The problem, of course, is what happens when worlds collide and it begins to dawn on us that God's grace is not a political commodity, nor are we called to live exclusively according to the patterns and practices of the world we are part of. Naaman's disorientation in the midst of that collision could be our own disorientation as we find that we are living in a collision between the world of kings and the world of the kingdom, one equipped well to maintain price tags and contracts while the other possesses the power to be reconciled to God and to one another, to be healed at the point of our deepest need, so long as we are willing to accept the kingdom on its terms and step away from the temptation to try to buy grace. In the world of the kingdom, all attempts to buy what is being freely given are but an exercise in decorated irrelevance, for the kingdom's purpose is not to maintain distance between individuals but to bring people together under the banner of God's reconciliation. As that difference is seen and understood, kings do well to confess their inability to heal our deepest wounds.

Therefore, we would do well to accept the free grace of God. And as we do so, we would also do well to allow the receiving of that grace to challenge the assumptions that have long formed us about money, power, and the world of kings. God's offering of grace freely is in no way an attempt to coax political favor. It is precisely the freeness of God's grace that turns the world of kings on its head. As free grace encounters a system built on the need to win favor through financial maneuvering, it explodes the expectations of those who walk to the rhythms of the world of kings. Like Naaman, they are disoriented when they encounter free grace. Yet it is precisely that free grace on which we depend to disorient us from the way we have been so deeply formed by the world of kings, and that disorientation of free grace is our hope for moving toward the world of the kingdom as we step out of the world of kings.

THE RECOUNT

The World of Kings:	The World of the Kingdom:
Cannot seem to hear the voices of the powerless and meek	Hears the voices of the powerless and meek, taking them seriously
Understands favor to come with a price tag, making bartering for favor a necessary part of political life	Understands favor and grace to be offered freely, making barter unnecessary
Understands power as something that needs to be bought	Understands that power is not only freely bestowed but also used to bring about reconciliation
Thinks of people as individuals, making contracts the primary way through which agreements are made	Understands people to be connected to one another, and values the trust that being connected fosters

THE ECONOMICS OF PLENTY

2 KINGS 6:8–7:2

THE PASSAGE OF 2 KINGS 6:24–7:2 does not often come up in sermons or devotional readings. It's one that certainly doesn't show up in children's story Bibles, and it's not one of those stories that gets a lot of play in VBS curricula. In fact, when we dealt with this particular passage with our own congregation, we offered to buy anyone's lunch who could tell us truthfully that they had heard a sermon preached on this passage before. So far, no one has taken us up on the offer.

This is a passage, however, that opens up some beautiful insights about one of the most complex and tricky aspects of political life: economics. The way we view money, resources, and the acts of buying and selling are all wrapped together with the way we understand politics. Oftentimes, our economic philosophy drives our political outlook. It is good for us, then, to give ourselves to the narrative of 2 Kings 6, as difficult a story as it might be, to begin to understand the difference between a view of economics shaped by the world of kings and a view shaped by the world of the kingdom.

STEPPING INTO THE STORY

The story in front of us is a nightmarish tale of two women cooking and eating one of their children. As the writer of 2 Kings outlines, the Aramean army has surrounded Samaria, a city at the heart of the kingdom of Israel, where Elisha is staying and where much of his ministry probably takes place. We are told that a siege of Samaria by the army of Aram has cut off whatever food supply there was. The lack of food is so severe that the residents of Samaria take to eating things like donkey heads and bird dung—and those items actually fetch a decent price at market! There is a subtext here as well. As awful as it is to consider, during normal economic times, the poor have likely already been eating things like donkey heads and bird dung. As a food shortage sets in and the Samarian economy is turned on its head, donkey heads and bird dung are now being sold for a high price, leaving the poor with nothing to eat. And when you have nothing to eat, desperation can lead to impossible choices.

As the king walks along the wall of the city, a woman screams to him for help. She tells him a chilling story about a deal she made with a friend: They would eat this woman's child one day and the other woman's child the next day. We can't be quite sure of how they went about deciding whose child to eat first, but what we do know is that they finally decided to eat this woman's son. Her complaint to the king is that, when the next day came and it was the second woman's turn to fulfill her end of the deal, she suddenly lost track of her son; he is conveniently nowhere to be found.

The horror and injustice of what he has just heard is too much for the king, whose only response to the woman is to tear his clothing and call for the execution of Elisha, presumably because the king is convinced that Elisha—the man of God—is the only person in the city who can do something about their situation, and he has apparently done nothing. As the king dispatches a messenger to Elisha, we are told that the prophet has a fairly good idea of what is about to take place. His message to the messenger, then, is this: *By this time tomorrow, everything will change. Not only will the famine be lifted, but the entire donkey-head-and-bird-dung economy is going to turn around for the better.*

This is a strange story, indeed, and still it is part of that great story of God's faithfulness that helps us glimpse the political and economic realities of the world around us with a new imagination. One thing we ought to notice right away is that the king of Israel is not named. Through historical investigation, we can probably surmise who this king actually is, but that would be an exercise in missing the point. The writer of 2 Kings has chosen not to name the king, suggesting that this king is no one; he is every king. By not naming the king, the writer reinforces the king's own message to the woman who cries out to him for help: "If the LORD does not help you, where can I get help for you?" (2 Kings 6:27). The name the king uses for God here is not generic. It is Yahweh, the proper and holy name of God. Therefore, the unnamed king, who apparently cannot save the woman, names the God who can. By not naming the king, the writer of 2 Kings makes a theological point: Who will be the salvation of the people in this situation?

At the same time, we might also catch hints here that in not naming this particular king, the writer may be suggesting that this could be any king. There's something here that hints at the *office* of king, more than the particular person who happens to be filling the office at that time. In not naming the king, the writer may want us to see a reality here that is true of kings in general, so he leaves out this king's name, that we might see that this king does what many kings do.

Of course, there are other kings of Israel who are named, whose particular names we do remember, and whose names come immediately to mind as we encounter the story of two feuding woman and one dead child: Solomon, for instance. We remember his name because we remember him as a great king who ruled Israel during a time of peace and prosperity. The reason his leadership was successful was never meant to be a secret. Solomon asked God for wisdom. Solomon's fabled wisdom is known in his own kingdom as well as in neighboring kingdoms. First Kings 3 gives us the story of what happens immediately after Solomon asks for wisdom. God's answer comes in the form of a woman bringing a complaint to the king. In a very similar way that we might bring a case before a judge, kings in Solomon's time often heard cases and rendered judgments.

In this particular case the woman's complaint is that she and her housemate are having a dispute over a baby. Both women gave birth to babies around the same time, and now there are multiple children of the same age in the house. Sometime during the night, the woman's housemate rolled over on her own baby, leading to the child's death. The housemate, not wanting to lose everything that comes with having a child, switched the children in the night, exchanging a live child for a dead one. But mothers know their children, and when the woman awoke in the morning and saw that the dead child lying beside her was not her child, she knew what had happened.

Now, standing before Solomon, she pleads her case, though her housemate denies what she did, leading to a classic case of she-said/she-said. Solomon's well-known response is to order that his sword be brought to him, announcing that he will cut the child in half and each woman can take one half of the child. Of course, the real mother of the child reacts to save the life of her child, even if that means having him raised by someone else, and at the moment of her reaction, Solomon is able to render his verdict: She is the true mother of the child. "When all Israel heard the verdict the king had given, they held the king in awe, because they saw that he had wisdom from God to administer justice" (1 Kings 3:28). Solomon can see things no one else can see, and that kind of vision has the people of Israel in awe of their king.

We ought to have Solomon in mind when we encounter 2 Kings 6 because, though these stories are incredibly similar, they are also incredibly different, and that may be precisely the point. Each of these kings handles each situation differently, and we ought to take note of those differences. One can see; the other cannot.

The ability to see something that others cannot is a running theme in 1 and 2 Kings. In 2 Kings 6, one of the things that sets Elisha apart as a man of God is his ability to see where Aram, the nemesis of Israel in those days, is going to send a raiding force. Beyond that, Elisha is able to see that the Aramean army isn't to be feared because there are forces working alongside the Israelite army that no one else is really quite able to see, until God allows it. Verses 15-16 give us this incredible insight: "When the servant of the man of God got up and went out early the next morning, an army with horses and chariots had surrounded the city. 'Oh no, my lord! What shall we do?' the servant asked. 'Don't be afraid,' the prophet answered. 'Those who are with us are more than those who are with them.'" Elisha then prays for the servant to see what he sees, and as he does, the servant is able to see the hills filled with horses and chariots, a powerful military force that outnumbers the attacking Aramean army.

Beyond the servant being given the ability to see, Elisha prays for the Aramean army's sight to be taken away, and the entire army is struck with blindness so Elisha can go to them, tell them they are going the wrong direction, and lead them through the gates of Samaria and into Israel's military citadel. The ability to see is the difference between the Arameans being an attacking force and prisoners of war. After their vision is restored and they realize they have just walked into the enemy capital and are now at the mercy of Israel, Elisha asks that they not be killed but fed and sent on their way, back to Aram.

We can't miss the distinction here between those who can see and those who cannot see. Elisha can see, and he can see the ways that God is quietly working for the salvation of Israel. He can see when God is moving and working to protect God's people, even when it doesn't really look like salvation.

When we come to the story of the siege, then, we can already see that the writer of 2 Kings is making a powerful distinction: Elisha can see; the king cannot. When we find the king, he is walking on top of the wall, most likely to inspect the military situation. He is probably looking at the enemy positions to see if there is any shortcoming or soft spot in their lines that he can exploit for the good of his own people. In other words, he has climbed to a place where he can see everything, and we begin to realize he can actually see nothing.

Consider for a moment the distinction between the two conflicts involving Samaria in 2 Kings 6. In the first, Elisha responds out of his ability to see what God is doing to save and preserve God's people. His actions follow his ability to see God's salvation because that is precisely what he is looking for. In the second, however, the king seems to be kept from seeing the same things Elisha saw. Rather than God's salvation, he only sees an overwhelming enemy and his own inability to save his people. At that point, a poor woman, who likely would never be given a formal audience with a king, stands at the base of the wall and demands that he listen to her.

"Help me, my lord the king!" she cries, though another possible translation of the Hebrew word she uses (*yasha*) could be, "Save me" (2 Kings 6:26).

The king's response to her supplication is surprisingly theological. "If the LORD does not help you, where can I get help for you? From the threshing floor? From the winepress" (2 Kings 6:27)?

The king pauses. And then, he opens court. "What's the matter?" His question is essentially permission for a hearing to be convened, for him to take up his role as king and render judgment on the issue the woman has brought. As the heinous details of her situation unfold, you can imagine that a hush might fall over the city. If you've ever had the kind of moment when you hear or see something so jarring that it immediately changes everything, you can relate to the kind of moment that is unfolding along the city wall. In those moments when you hear something so horrifying, the whole world seems as if it stops revolving for a second.

And in that moment, the people of Israel are, in some sense, forced to share this woman's shame. They are made to take on her shame as their very own king, in all his might and authority, is forced to admit that he is powerless to do anything about this situation. The king, again, is decorated irrelevance. There is nothing that even the king can do for this woman who is so hungry she has been driven to the most desperate of places. He can't see another way out.

We are clearly not dealing with a Solomon in this situation. Rather than appeal to God for wisdom, rather than appeal to God to be able to see things that others can't see, this king resorts to blaming God, indicting Elisha and ordering his execution. As far as this king is concerned, the whole situation can be laid at the feet of the man of God. Elisha will pay for this horror, and everyone can blame God for the pain of the whole city.

Remember that 1 and 2 Kings were written during a time of exile for Israel. When we read 2 Kings, we read it as the things that actually happened in Israel's history, but we also read it with the understanding that Israel's present circumstance causes certain aspects of these stories to stand out in particular ways. Because they are living in exile, we can't help but think that the king's response would stand out to people in the midst of a painful political situation. Their homeland has been taken from them, along with their forms of governance and their entire way of life. We can imagine that in those bleak moments punctuated by loss and pain, it would become very easy to blame God. In the same way that the king's recourse is to become angry with God, we suspect that a people living through an incredibly painful political season in the history of their nation would be tempted to do the same. The message here should cut through: When you don't have a vision for the way God is saving in the midst of hardship, your recourse will be to blame God and sink into despair. You can either ask God to help you see something others can't, or you can blame God for your circumstances.

STEPPING INTO THE KINGDOM

Of course, there are political and economic implications here as well. This is a story that challenges us to examine the kind of vision we have as we approach the very real circumstances of life that deal with things like war, poverty, and hunger. The contrast between Elisha's vision and the king's vision challenges us to examine the way our political vision has been shaped. Are we focusing on the present circumstances to the point that our vision becomes narrow? When we take into account the king, standing on a wall of the city, we suppose he ought to have a wide vision from his vantage point, but his ability to see anything beyond the immediate situation is telling of his political vision. From where he is, all his vision is downward. He looks down at the enemy soldiers. He looks down upon the woman. But not once does he stop to consider looking up. His vision for dealing with the situation is completely caught up in the immediacy of the situation, of how to get through *this* day.

Obviously, there are political realities that need immediate attention. People cannot wait to eat. Injustice must be addressed and stopped. We aren't suggesting that our political strategy should be, "Look up and wait." Rather, part of what 2 Kings teaches us is that the world of kings would have us be consumed by a narrow political vision that cannot see beyond the immediacy of the situation. The world of kings would suggest to us that life is primarily about *this* moment of pain and suffering; that the right course of action is that which allows us to do what we need to simply survive *this* situation, rather than take a larger view of what particular political decisions may do to us as a people. The world of kings does not require that we have Elisha's vision. It doesn't require that we lift our heads. Rather, it would have us believe that the immediate problem is all that matters, so if we allow ourselves to be persuaded by the world of kings, our vision becomes small. Like the king, our gaze is downcast.

Old Testament scholar Walter Brueggemann has written on the distinction he sees throughout Scripture between what he calls the myth of scarcity and the liturgy of abundance.[18] The liturgy (a word that literally means "the work of the people") of abundance,

---

18. Walter Brueggemann, "The Liturgy of Abundance, the Myth of Scarcity," *Christian Century* (March 24-31, 1999).

Brueggemann demonstrates, is woven into Scripture from the beginnings of Genesis. The narratives of creation not only demonstrate the kind of relationship a creative God has with a good creation but also that the God who creates does so out of overwhelming abundance. When God speaks of the way the creation will provide food for the creatures, it is in the mode of complete abundance: "I give you every seed-bearing plant on the face of the whole earth and every tree that has fruit with seed in it. They will be yours for food" (Genesis 1:29). Notice that, by virtue of bearing seeds, even the food God is giving contains the potential for producing more food! Therefore, God's command to be fruitful and multiply needn't be a frightful stress on the natural resources of creation because the very confession of God as creator contains within it the affirmation that God has created in abundance. From top to bottom, the biblical affirmation of God's creative impulse screams, "There is plenty!"

When God's people read these words, when we rehearse the deep and subtle beauty they convey about who God is, when we allow them to shape us and authoritatively persuade our coming and our going, they become the liturgy of our lives, or the way we go about our work in the world. We do well to remember that the power of liturgy is when it takes hold of us during our acts of worshiping God and spills out into and over a broken world. When we gather for worship, the words we read from Scripture, the stories we tell one another of God's faithfulness, the truths we proclaim in song, and the way we hear the gospel proclaimed are not meant to be contained to the church building. They are meant to form the way we see ourselves and the way we see the world so that the same patterns we learn in our worship are replicated in the world. When we practice a liturgy of abundance week in and week out in our worship gatherings, we learn how to practice a liturgy of abundance at work, in our political associations, and even in the way we participate in political economy and economic exchange.

However, Brueggemann points out that it doesn't take long before humans dismiss the liturgy of abundance in favor of the myth of scarcity. The myth of scarcity is simply, "There is not enough." A vision of life that sees food, time, money, and resources as scarce is the kind of vision that quickly looks away from a God of abundance and tells us that the worship of a God who provides is a waste when what we ought to be doing is working as hard as we can to secure as many of the scarce resources for ourselves as we can before others take them from us. Brueggemann identifies Genesis 47 as one of the first times in the Bible that the myth of scarcity appears. "In that chapter, Pharaoh dreams that there will be a famine in the land. So Pharaoh gets organized to administer, control, and monopolize the food supply. Pharaoh introduces the principle of scarcity into the world economy. For the first time in the Bible, someone says, 'There's not enough. Let's get everything.'"[19]

The myth that starts with Pharaoh echoes through 2 Kings, resonating in the ears of the unnamed Israelite king, and closing his eyes to the possibilities of enough. It's no mistake that the myth of scarcity originates in the biblical text through one who is firmly embedded in the world of kings, and what we see in 2 Kings 6 is that kings are still operating according to the same myth: *There is not enough.*

Famine, lack, and scarcity can quickly consume our vision. They can quickly obscure the way we see God's plentitude in the world, and can convince us that if we are to be cared for, if we are going to get enough to eat, it must be according to the rules and rhythms of the world of kings. As we've seen in the story of the woman who has eaten her own child, her vision is so impacted by the myth of scarcity that it leads her to literally devour her hope for the future because all she can see is lack.

---

19. Brueggemann, "The Liturgy of Abundance, the Myth of Scarcity," 1999.

If we think that the myth of scarcity is a political reality constrained to the pages of the Bible, we only need to check the headlines and ask what kind of political motivations are driving stories having to do with hot-button issues such as immigration, for instance. Why is it that, even though we are commanded to welcome the stranger, we are so averse to doing so? In many cases, it comes down to this myth: *There will not be enough for me if I allow you to share.* Though immigration politics are complex and therefore outside the scope of this chapter, we can also say that both sides of the current immigration debate, to some degree, have their basis in the fear that comes when our vision has been shaped by the myth of scarcity. We cannot ignore that the majority of the motivation for immigration throughout history has been and still is economic, and deeply tied to a lack of adequate resources.

In the North American context, ten million Mexican citizens are living both legally and illegally in the United States—nearly 10 percent of Mexico's population.[20] Economist Joseph Stiglitz sees this staggering statistic and points to a common Mexican phrase close to the heart of immigration motivations: "Mexico—so far from God, so close to the United States."[21] Though his use of the phrase is meant to point to many of the economic motivations for North American migration patterns, it also points to some of the theological vision underlying the politics of immigration. Embedded in this little phrase is the idea that when one is close to God, one is also close to provision. That theological idea is not well at home in the world of the kingdom, though it is in the world of kings. According to the vision of the world of kings, if God is not providing resources, God must

---

20. OECD, *OECD Economic Surveys*, "OECD Economic Surveys Mexico: Migration: The Economic Context and Implications," vol. 2003, no. 1 (Paris: OECD, 2003), 152-212.

21. Joseph E. Stiglitz, *Making Globalization Work* (New York: W.W. Norton and Company, 2007), 61.

be at a distance, and as such, we must take matters into our own hands in the face of scarcity. If we hear this, however, and come to believe that this is some kind of critique upon those who choose to take matters into their own hands by attempting a dangerous journey of migration, we haven't heard 2 Kings. In the same way that we don't blame the woman for the situation leading her to devour her son, we also do not blame the poor for their lack of resources. As we encounter 2 Kings, we are challenged to carefully begin to examine a political vision deeply shaped by the world of kings, especially as that vision begins to form a political and economic reality influenced by the myth of scarcity.

One of the most insidious aspects of a political vision formed by the myth of scarcity is that it not only erodes faith in God's provision, but it does so to the detriment of generous and faithful stewardship. If we are convinced by the myth of scarcity, if we live according to its rhythms and political patterns, our vision will eventually come to be like that of the king, who has a narrow vision, who can only see the lack. When all we can see is lack, we are far less likely to give. In fact, we are all the more likely to consume to indiscriminate excess.

Pointing to the results of a sociological study on stewardship conducted at Princeton University, Brueggemann lays out the connection between our theological vision of plentitude and our practices of stewardship. "Though many of us are well-intentioned," he writes, "we have invested our lives in consumerism. We have a love affair with 'more'—and we will never have enough."[22]

The myth of scarcity motivates us to take more than we need and to consume beyond what faithful stewardship would allow. That is, since our political and economic visions have been so shaped by the fear that there will not be enough for us, we do all we can to be sure that there will always be enough for us, even if that means tak-

---

22. Brueggemann, "The Liturgy of Abundance, the Myth of Scarcity," 1999.

ing more than we need to the detriment of others, or engaging in purchasing patterns that clearly favor our well-being over that of the person who has provided that good to us. Second Kings challenges the idea that getting the lowest price for something is automatically a good thing because, if the highest good of a purchase is that we are getting the most resource for the least cost while paying no attention to what it costs others for us to pay an unreasonably low price, we are probably more formed by the myth of scarcity than we realize.

A vision formed primarily to see lack rather than plentitude is often not equipped to see the possibilities for provision that can take place through exchanges. So long as we see only lack, economic exchange will be turned to the mode of getting the most for ourselves, no matter the cost to others. Alternatively, if we are able to see the plentitude of God, could it be that our economic activity could actually be a means of allowing others to share in that plentitude?

Theologian and ethicist Oliver O'Donovan developed the biblical concept of *koinonia*, commonly translated as "community" in an economic sense, suggesting that the church is the body in which the members communicate the goods of God's creation to one another. For O'Donovan, communication doesn't have as much to do with transmitting information and ideas to one another as it has to do with forging an economic middle ground between *yours* and *mine*. As he sees it, "to 'communicate' is to hold some thing as common, to make it a common possession, to treat it as 'ours,' rather than 'yours' or 'mine.'"[23] O'Donovan's economic suggestion here is thoroughly theological: It is to steward our resources as if they are on loan to us from God, and to believe that God is the one who has provided them and that they ought to be treated as such. When we begin to believe we have exclusive lordship over material goods, we exclude the lordship of God.

---

23. Oliver O'Donovan, *The Ways of Judgment* (Grand Rapids: Wm. B. Eerdmans Publishing Co., 2005), 242.

When we enter into the activity of buying and selling, then, O'Donovan challenges us to see that activity as far more than getting something for ourselves. Rather, it is an opportunity to relate to the person with whom we are entering into relationship through the act of buying or selling. Market exchange, or the act of buying and selling, in O'Donovan's view, opens the door for us to communicate the goods of God's creation to one another and to allow the other person to flourish in a way that he or she could not have been capable of before. This is not to say that private ownership of material and money disappears, but it is to suggest that we have a different vision of the *purpose* of our ownership of those materials. They are not given to us to be exploited but to be stewarded with the kingdom of God at the forefront of our vision.

If we are honest about our activity of buying and selling, we will probably come to the conclusion that our vision of those activities has been deeply shaped by the world of kings. We have been formed to believe that the act of buying and selling ought to be primarily for our benefit. We buy things when we think we've found a low price, and we don't consider the cost to the seller. We sell when we believe we can receive a high payout, rarely considering the cost to the buyer. If we pause to consider the words to describe economic exchange, we can see that we assign goodness to the act of exchange based on what we get: "I found a good price" means that I didn't have to pay very much. "I got a good price" means that someone paid us an amount that is to our benefit. The point here is not that we ought to only buy and sell to our detriment; rather, we ought to consider using a different metric to measure whether an act of economic exchange is "good." Using a different metric will usually require that we adjust our vision.

If we are going to consider an act of economic exchange to be good when its outcome is to be a blessing to both parties, it will require us to have a vision of economics that is formed by the world of the kingdom. It will require us to see God's plentitude where others may see lack. It will require us to see the goods entrusted to us as belonging to God and to be used according to God's purposes, all while remembering that the same God who has entrusted material goods to our care is the God who created in an act of sheer plentitude, making the garden of Eden "the space where God and humankind are to be at home together."[24]

A vision of God's plentitude can transform the purpose we give to economic exchange. So long as our vision is formed by only seeing lack, the purpose of economic exchange will be to benefit ourselves, even if it is painful and costly to others. According to the world of kingdoms, this is quite simply the way economies work. From a perspective of plentitude, however, our economic exchanges take on a new purpose that is forever at home in the world of the kingdom. This purpose is to communicate the goods of God's creation to those who are experiencing a very real lack of provision in the midst of very real circumstances.

We cannot be naïve about the actual lack of resources that many people in the world experience and struggle with on a daily basis. We cannot say that lack of clean drinking water and adequate food supply are simply circumstances they ought not to fixate upon. Many of the causes of lack of proper stewardship of resources can be traced back to the myth of scarcity, a myth that flourishes when one's vision has been shaped by the world of kings.

A large part of what this chapter is asking is, What is economic provision *for*? What is its purpose? What is it meant to do? The way we answer this question will, in many ways, help us come to terms with the grotesque nature of this story and the questions that might be plaguing us about why God didn't act sooner so a mother didn't have to eat her own child.

By now, we should see that the writer of 2 Kings loves to put people, places, and stories alongside one another as a telling comparison,

---

24. O'Donovan, *The Ways of Judgment*, 245.

and chapter 6 is no different. Just after we hear about the woman petitioning the king for a word of justice, just after we see how the king's vision has become increasingly small, we see how Elisha responds to the same situation with a vision that hasn't been formed by the world of kings but by the world of the kingdom. The comparison between these two visions, though, is exactly the point we need to be picking up in 2 Kings 6.

The king's vision has been formed by the world of kings. His options are to go to war against a superior army or fall into despair. Sadly, his narrow vision has an impact on those in his city. The woman sees her options as letting the king save them, or falling into despair, literally swallowing all hope for the future. Elisha, however, comes to the situation with a vision shaped by the world of the kingdom. Granted, the world of the kingdom looks different from the world of kings. Its hope is different. Its view of the world is different. And its view of God's provision is different.

Considering the different visions represented in this story, we might begin to ask how economic provision functions according to each outlook. What is provision *for* in the world of kings? It's likely that the king is not considering this question as he paces the walls of his city, looking out at the military blockade that is starving his city to death. What is provision for? It is to feed people. It is to be sure they have what they need so they don't wither and die.

According to the woman's vision, it may be helpful to consider what provision is for. In her case, it may be for the preservation of herself and her son. In this vision, provision has a relatively small circle of influence. It is for us, or for me. But in the world of kings, economic provision is rarely *for* anything other than yourself. As we have seen before in 2 Kings, kings will go to battle over provisions because they want to benefit their own kingdoms.

In the world of the kingdom, however, economic provision takes on a different purpose. God's people can see economic goods as something to be used for divine purposes rather than simply for their own benefit. In the world of kings, provision is intended for consumption. In the world of the kingdom, provision is intended for salvation. The problem with the economic vision of the world of kings, however, is that if economic provision is meant for me to consume, there will never be enough. I will always have my head over my shoulder, wondering if someone else is going to take what I have. I will always see lack. If economic provision serves the purpose of bald consumption, there will never be enough. If, however, it serves God's purposes of salvation, we must recognize that God's plentitude has always been and will continue to be superabundant. The rhythm and logic of the world of the kingdom see economic provision not as something to be consumed but as something to be stewarded for the good purposes of God's redemption. And if there's anything we know about God, it is that God has never skimped on providing for the salvation of God's people.

Given these competing visions, it should not surprise us that the king is dressed in sackcloth, the garb of those who mourn. It shouldn't shock us that the woman came to such a point of despair that she went to extreme lengths. If economic salvation is not apparent according to the rhythm and logic of the world of kings, despair is actually a fairly logical response. After all, according to the world of kings, economic provision is here to benefit *me*. If I am not being benefited, the economic situation is broken, and despair is probably my only option.

But it also should not surprise us that Elisha's vision is able to expand beyond the despair of the woman and the king, even as he is counted among them as one who is affected by the siege. If provision is *for* God's redemptive purposes, God will do what God needs to do, according to Elisha's vision. Granted, Elisha is vague on the details of how this provision will occur, but he is exceedingly clear that God will do what needs to be done so that God's promises of salvation and redemption will not be overcome by those things that threaten the promise.

As Elisha proclaims the faithfulness of God in stating that provision will arrive by the next day, one of the king's most trusted officers balks at the idea, responding in complete accordance with the world of kings: "Look, even if the LORD should open the floodgates of the heavens, could this happen" (2 Kings 7:2)?

The officer's remarks, from the ground up, are an exercise in missing the point. He, like the king above him, has been so thoroughly formed to see economic provision in terms of benefiting himself that he can't conceive of provision being used for the purposes of divine salvation. Perhaps this is what prompts Elisha's response to the king's officer: "'You will see it with your own eyes,' answered Elisha, 'but you will not eat any of it!'" (2 Kings 7:2). There is a curious significance in Elisha's words if God's provision is indeed purposed for God's redemption, and not simply for our consumption. With the vision of the world of the kingdom in mind, Elisha's message might be, "You will see God's provision for the sake of God's kingdom, but you won't taste it." In other words, God's provisions are meant to be used for God's redemptive purposes, but if you can't see them as such, you won't be able to enjoy the fullness of what those provisions can be.

How will we see God's provision? Will it be in terms of material goods meant to benefit our own consumption? If so, we may often be faced with the darkness of despair when we believe there is not enough. Or, we may be able to see the abundance of God's provision with our own eyes while being incapable of experiencing the fullness of what God's provision has always been intended to be: the means of righteousness, justice, and healing in the world.

The competing visions in 2 Kings 6 also point to a political challenge. We will engage differently, in a political sense, if our vision of economic provision has been shaped according to one world or the other. In the 2008 U.S. presidential election, economic questions became the chief concern of a majority of the electorate. By 2012, the economy still drove much of the political rhetoric. But what drove these economic concerns was lack. Scarcity. Fear. The belief that there would not be enough for *me*. As each of the major candidates made their appeals to the people, the message was essentially the same: "I can eliminate the lack better than the other guy can. I can save you from scarcity. If you elect me, there will be enough for you." The problem with this idea, illuminated by 2 Kings 6, is that as long as we believe that economic provision is meant exclusively for our private consumption, there will never be enough, no matter whom we elect. A vision of plentitude comes only as we begin to understand that provision is God's gift, intended to be used for God's purposes.

An economic vision shaped by the world of kings would have us see economic provision according to our desire to consume, according to what provision can do for us. But what if it isn't about us? What if it is more about God's protection of the promise to redeem the world? What if things like politics and economics are less about meeting our needs and more about living into the reality of God's kingdom coming "on earth as it is in heaven"? A vision of economic life according to the world of the kingdom is not to benefit ourselves at the expense of the other; it is for both parties to flourish because the exchange is characterized by the goods of God's creation being faithfully and non-exploitatively communicated among those who are exchanging.

The same is true in a larger political sense. Rather than measure the goodness of a particular political action according to how it benefits us, what if we began to measure the good of that political action according to the way it allows God's redemption of creation to take better hold in our world? In many ways, we can see this challenge being issued to us in 2 Kings 6. If the goodness of this story is measured only according to the rubric of benefiting the individuals in the narrative, it doesn't seem to pass the test. We may be saying to ourselves, *Why doesn't Elisha act sooner? Why doesn't God act sooner? Why does a mother need to endure the loss of hope and these horrific circumstances? Why does an innocent child need to lose his life? This story can't possibly be good!* But if we measure the goodness of this story according to the way God's promise for the salvation of creation is protected, we may be able to find an alternative vision of provision that is established on the hope that God has always provided what God's people need to be faithful, rather than turning to despair because we have come to believe that God's provision is there to meet the ends of our consumption. One of these visions will lead us to cry out to the king to save us by providing more for us to consume. The other will lead us to offer our thanks for the way God's provision for the salvation of the world has always come to us in abundance.

Indeed, God's provision has included God's own self, poured out for us in abundance for the sake of our salvation. If we remember the woman's cry to the king, "Save us!" or, *yasha* in Hebrew, it begins to trigger something in our memories, be it ever so slight, that there is another woman who has a son, who calls out something very similar. Matthew 1 records the word that will be called out after another young mother gives birth to a son: *Yeshua*. If they sound similar, they should; they both have saving at the heart of their meaning. In the case of the woman in 2 Kings 6, she cries out *yasha*, or "save us!" while Mary, mother of Jesus, calls her son *Yeshua*, which means "he will save." One woman demands to be saved by a king, having seen only lack. The other marvels that her baby *is* the king, and in him she sees bountiful, though unexpected, plentitude and provision. The challenge for us is this: Will our vision be so narrow that we can only imagine salvation coming to us at the hands of the king, according to the rhythm and logic of the world of kings? Or will we allow our vision to be expanded according to the rhythms and logic of the world of the kingdom, that we would see salvation not in a powerful king but in a helpless child?

THE RECOUNT

The World of Kings:	The World of the Kingdom:
Provisions are meant for my consumption	Provisions are meant for God's redemption
I must compete for provisions	I receive provisions as a gift
There will never be enough	God has always provided enough in all things necessary to our salvation
I see lack	I see plentitude

THE SANCTIFIED VISION OF THE KINGDOM

2 KINGS 7:3-20

TIM REALLY ENJOYED TRIPS to the optometrist when he was a kid. His optometrist was an avid collector of frog figurines, so from every corner and from behind every decorative plant, a pair of amphibian eyes looked back at you. The doctor also used frog figurines in his exams, and Tim loved being able to see which new ones had been added to the collection each time he went back for an appointment.

There were also the video games. No other type of doctor could compete with that. As part of the eye exams, the peripheral vision test included placing your head in what amounted to an up-turned colander and taking hold of a clicker in your hand, like a contestant on a game show. The instructions were to look straight ahead, and each time you saw a flash or blur of light to the side, you were to press the button. It was a challenge, and it was a lot more fun than anything that ever happened at the dentist's office.

All of those eye tests, in one way or another, test whether we can see the world rightly. There are tests to be sure that things are in focus, that things are clear, and that things are right-side up. One of the keys to approaching the political world as a Christian is to see the political world differently. In essence, it's to see the political world upside down. That is the first step toward seeing the world with sanctified vision.

Sanctification is a word derived from Latin that simply means "to make something holy." There are lots of ways we can approach what it means to be holy, and there are lots of other books that have been written on that subject. But for our purposes here, *to be made holy* is simply this: to be set apart for God's purposes alone.

There's a lot of good news for us in 2 Kings 7, especially in terms of how we can navigate highly charged political times as people who seek to be faithful to God. But it's going to take a sanctified vision for us to be able to see that good news.

STEPPING INTO THE STORY

In the final stop in this journey through the beginning chapters of 2 Kings, we pick up where we left off at the end of chapter 6 and the opening verses of chapter 7. As you may remember, 2 Kings 6 gives us the story of Samaria being trapped by a siege, with the opposing army blocking all means of bringing in food. Families resort to eating anything they can find—even their own children. In the midst of this horror, a woman cries out to the king, who is walking along the top of the wall, for justice. "If the LORD does not help you, where can I get help for you?" comes the king's response (2 Kings 6:27). It is a good thought, and the king turns to Elisha, who speaks for God in telling the king that flour and barley—precious commodities in very short supply—will be so plentiful by the next day that their prices will drop and everyone in the city will be able to afford them.

The king's advisor scoffs at the idea. "Look, even if the Lord should open the floodgates of the heavens, could this happen?" he asks (2 Kings 7:2). Economies are too big to turn in a day, and economies depend on supply, which sometimes takes even longer to turn.

"You will see it with your own eyes," says Elisha in response, "but you will not eat any of it!" (2 Kings 7:2).

The writer of 2 Kings immediately takes us to a story of four men with leprosy, a technique we now recognize as the writer's attempt to set stories alongside one another for the sake of comparison. Faced with a difficult decision between entering the city—which is not only illegal for them but also foolish during a siege—and turning themselves over to the Aramean army, they opt for the choice that doesn't end in certain death. By turning themselves over to the Arameans, at least they have a slight chance of survival; entering the city will lead to nothing good for them.

The author of the story suddenly becomes intent on telling us details about the time of day these things are taking place. In the case of the leprous men turning themselves over to the Arameans, it's happening at dusk, a detail that has a lot to do with how well people can see. Rather than turn themselves over in full daylight, when vision is at its best, they go as the light gives way to darkness. No one should be able to see well in those conditions.

Arriving at the camp of the Arameans, they discover a lot of empty tents—the remnants of an army running away in fear from the sounds of approaching attackers. The writer of 2 Kings tells us that God has caused the Arameans to hear the sounds of an approaching army. Again, we are told that they left at dusk, when vision is fading. Part of this may have to do with the actual physical conditions, but we shouldn't miss out on the theological point the author is making: Clear sight leads to good actions.

When these four men, making one last, desperate attempt at survival, arrive at the camp and find a trove of food and supplies, the feast is on. They help themselves to food, drink, clothes, and money. Their feasting, though, quickly leads to guilt. They reason among themselves that the absence of the Aramean army is essentially the news of salvation for everyone in the city, and that this good news is not meant to be kept to themselves. "If we wait until daylight," they say to one another, "punishment will overtake us. Let's go at once and report this to the royal palace" (2 Kings 7:9). The exact nature of the punishment they fear isn't altogether clear, but we do get an unambiguous sense that waiting to share this news would not be a good thing. Again, we see that the author of 2 Kings wants to make a point about vision: If the men wait until everyone can see clearly, it won't be good.

Approaching the walls of the city, these men essentially become the eyes of all who live in the city, as well as the king. In the dark of night, they alone are the ones who can clearly see the salvation being offered to an entire city that is literally starving to death.

Approaching the city, though, is a bold act for anyone who has leprosy. The laws of the day prohibit those with leprosy to have any kind of contact with those in the city, for fear of spreading the disease to others. But now, these men have some good news to spread. The question in front of us is whether the king will be able to see in the dark, especially if his eyes are four leprous men—outcasts from the city. The question of vision immediately springs back into our memories; Elisha's ominous warning to the king's lieutenant begins to take on new meaning as we are now confronted with men who are able to see in the dark.

STEPPING INTO THE KINGDOM

Tim remembers a fun conversation he had with a teenager in our church who was helping him stock the food pantry with recently donated bags of canned goods after a Thanksgiving dinner. Somehow, the topic of holiness came up in their conversation, and between sorting the green beans from the chicken noodle soup, they had a pretty decent theological conversation. Tim asked her if she knew what made something holy. She pointed to the hole in the knee of her jeans. "No, but my jeans do," she joked. Over the next few minutes, they chatted about being set totally apart for God's purposes. They talked about the things we call holy.

The Bible was a good example. It's not that the Bible is printed on holy paper, or that it's printed with holy ink or even put together in a holy binding. The Bible is holy because it's set apart as a special body of literature the sole purpose of which is to pass along the good news of God's salvation. The Bible isn't a mechanical manual meant to show you how to fix something; it isn't a scientific journal meant to discuss the latest findings; and it isn't a romance novel meant to arouse the affections of a longing heart (though there are some sections that might qualify). In its entirety, the Bible is set apart for God's purposes. It doesn't truly do anything other than proclaim God's salvation. Tim's food-packing companion thought about that for a while before saying with intense intentionality, "Well, then I can be holy." We couldn't agree with her more.

If holiness is simply being set apart for God's purposes, then our political vision can be made holy; it can be sanctified. The way in which we see the world can be transformed and turned upside down so that what we once saw as the primary factors in writing our story (power, might, etc.) are exposed as being bare and empty of significance. At the same time, though, we can also begin to see that those things we once saw as irrelevant—the humble, powerless, and insignificant things of the world—are precisely those things God uses to write our story. Remember, it's God's faithfulness to the powerless that writes our story, that advances the redemptive mission of God in the world.

A sanctified vision can see the world right-side up, and can resist the temptation to throw in our lot with the kings on the mountaintops. A sanctified vision can begin to see unique and surprising ways that God advances a mission of redemption in the world. And a sanctified vision can help us to see the really good news that comes through 2 Kings 7.

There are three perspectives, or visions, that we can see in this passage, and as we have already learned, the writer of 2 Kings loves to compare the visions of different people to bring out a message. In this story, there is the vision of the king, that of the king's servant, and that of the leprous men. First, the king's perspective is—you guessed it—unable to see the good news of God's salvation. It's significant that this all takes place at night, when vision is at its worst. The king, whom we saw in 2 Kings 6, has a penchant for walking along the top of the city walls because, from that vantage point, he is supposed to have a clear perspective. But as we see in this passage, it's difficult to see God's salvation and the story God is writing when your vision is so shaped by the world of kings that you believe salvation comes through political might and that kings can write history by their victories—political, military, or economic.

Kings tend to see things right-side up and in accordance with the rhythms and logic of the world of kings. If we are honest with ourselves, we might find that our vision has been shaped by the world of kings to the point that we think salvation can come through the political, economic, and military might of kingdoms. Kings tend to see the world in terms of power. They rarely see good news coming to them from lepers. For a king, especially from the top of the city wall, you can see good news approaching from a long way off. It's an army in your coalition, coming to destroy your opposition. There's no mistaking it: It's huge, it makes a lot of noise, and it's fairly destructive. Good news comes through trusted channels. An advisor, or a messenger dispatched from the front, with news that the battle is going in your favor, perhaps. But good news doesn't come through unsavory channels—like from lepers.

And so we find the king in the night, when his vision is dull, and he's not able to see the good news of God's salvation. All the king can see is a trap. "I will tell you what the Arameans have done to us. They know we are starving; so they have left the camp to hide in the countryside, thinking, 'They will surely come out, and then we will take them alive and get into the city'" (2 Kings 7:12). The incredibly good news of God's salvation is lost on him because he sees the world right-side up. When you see the world right-side up, it's awfully hard to see the news of salvation that comes in rather upside-down ways. When your vision has been deeply shaped by the world of kings, you can't readily see the good news coming from the world of the kingdom. Tragically, the king can't see salvation even when it is standing on his own doorstep. Where God offers salvation, all the king can see is a trick.

There's also the king's advisor, whom we met earlier. It's significant that he is not only a close, trusted advisor—so trusted, in fact, that he is the "officer on whose arm [the king] leans" (2 Kings 7:2, 17). It is likely that he and the king share a similar vision. Like the king, this officer has trouble seeing salvation when it comes. A scoffer at God's word in Elisha's mouth, the king's officer can't see when salvation is at hand, probably because that isn't the way things happen in a right-side-up political world, the story of which is shaped by military and economic forces. In an upside-down vision, however, Elisha can see God's faithfulness at hand, and his vision bears that difference.

The perspective of the men with leprosy is the perspective that fascinates us the most, however, because it gives us a good glimpse of how upside-down the kingdom of God can be. These men, outsiders to everyone around them, become the bearers of the news of God's salvation. You may already know that, in addition to being separate from the rest of the community, those with leprosy are also required by law to yell out to others approaching that they are unclean and that others should stay away from them. Therefore, lepers are certainly not included in the king's trusted advisors.

Part of seeing the world right-side up is to trust news that comes only from credible sources, not from the margins of society. And so this particular king, dismissing the message because of the messengers, completely misses the good news they deliver. The good news of God's salvation often comes to us in upside-down ways and in humble, unexpected ways. God has a long history of delivering good news in strange ways. God tends to use unexpected people, even those who are outsiders, to bring us good news. The question this brings to our minds is whether we are capable of hearing the good news of God's salvation that outsiders can bring to us, or if we are too conditioned to hear good news only from those we deem credible sources.

But sometimes in the church's history we have tended to struggle with something called legalism. We say that we—the holy ones—are on the inside and that our purpose is to get those who are outside into the inside. To be clear, bringing others into the community of grace called the church is a very good thing. But sometimes, seeing ourselves as the insiders and others as outsiders, particularly when our insider-ness means we don't engage in certain activities that the outsiders do, means that we think outsiders have nothing to say to us, or that God couldn't use them to deliver good news. That arrangement has much to do with a right-side-up view of the world. The world of kings operates according to the intelligence being delivered from insiders, while the world of the kingdom has a tendency to surprise us when the news of God's salvation comes from unexpected places.

Even though we love this message, it's still a difficult one for us to swallow. We grew up in the church, and if you've spent a lot of time around the church, you may have seen how we church folk can sometimes get accustomed to hearing good news in particular ways. We like to hear good news from people like, well, ourselves. We, the authors, weren't particularly rebellious kids growing up, we attended a Christian college, went to seminary, and did everything by the book. In other words, around the church, we're pretty much insiders. Don't get us wrong: We thank God for the grace that has been so present in our lives and for so many of the gifts we've received from the church. But we also wonder if, in our being so accustomed to listening to insiders like ourselves, we may be missing the good news of God's salvation that's being brought to us by outsiders. We wonder if even our desire to "do it right" becomes a kind of right-side-up vision in and of itself, to the point that we become like the king—blind to the salvation God brings because it's announced in such an upside-down way. If this sounds unsettling, we hope we can remember that God has a long history of speaking through those who don't quite fit, or who are considered outsiders.

That's why we love that outsiders become the bearers of good news in 2 Kings 7. It's yet another installment of God's pattern of delivering the news of redemption in new and surprising ways. We don't often trust outsiders to give us good news of God's salvation, but if we see this story with sanctified vision—to see that holiness is simply being set apart for God's purposes—we can see that God's mission of redeeming creation is advanced yet again by those who aren't at all considered holy by their neighbors.

The political implications here are challenging as well. So long as our vision is formed by the world of kings, we are going to be far more prone to trust the information and narratives from those who are on "our" side rather than the "other" side. As long as your vision is formed like the king's vision, it's going to make the good news of God's salvation difficult to see, an unsettling thought when we consider how much we might be missing. The question for us is: *Can God use someone with whom I disagree for the redemptive purposes? Can God use someone outside of my usual networks to proclaim God's work?* If the answer is yes (and it is), it would be to our kingdom benefit to adjust our vision so that the most dominant story we see is that of God's salvation history, no matter where it might occur, no matter through whom God chooses to speak. Could the channels of trust we have built up actually be stemming the flow of God's good news? How might those who are on the outside of our networks—distanced from us by race, class, gender, nationality, or political affiliation—be agents of proclaiming God's redemption in our midst? Would we see it, or would we be too formed by the world of kings to be able to see them as viable conduits of salvation news?

God often works through those on the outside to speak good news of salvation to those on the inside. The challenge comes as we consider whether those on the inside can see the salvation being offered to them, or if their vision has been so shaped by the world of kings that even salvation looks like some kind of trap.

Obviously, a good dose of humility will be required to make that kind of shift, and humility rarely comes easily when our vision has been formed by the world of kings. In the world of kings, being right tends to serve ourselves, while in the world of the kingdom, being right is only worthwhile so long as it serves the purpose of God's redemptive work in the world. According to the rhythms and logic of the world of the kingdom, winning an argument is never as important as capturing the vision of what God is up to in the world. Therefore, a sanctified vision holds together these two things: the desire to grow in holiness and an unyielding humility that doesn't allow us to overlook what God might be announcing through one who doesn't look like us, especially one who isn't as far down the road to holiness as we may be.

This, to be sure, is a course walked carefully. If we use the term *outsider* to describe those who have turned away from the grace God offers, we certainly don't want to continue to make them outsiders for the sake of our being insiders. But neither do we want to make our insider status a category that blinds us to the surprising ways God chooses to announce salvation. When our insider status becomes that which is used to prop up either ourselves or our political visions, or to hold others at a distance from the grace we now enjoy, we are likely missing the announcement of good news that comes in new and surprising ways.

Second Kings offers a bountiful trove of narratives that challenge us to correct our political vision to see according to the world of the kingdom, but the book of Revelation can also help us understand more fully the concept of a sanctified political vision. Both Revelation and 2 Kings challenge their readers to make a choice between two political worlds; the choice between the world of kings and the world of the kingdom does not become any less sharp in the 650 years that transpire between the writing of each book. At the same time, each book gives us the choice between these two visions and points us toward one that is more fulfilling to what we humans have been created to be and how we have been created to associate. Moving from 2 Kings to Revelation allows us to revisit many of the same themes through the reality of what God has done historically between writings of these two books: sending Jesus Christ, who is the risen King.

Revelation is a political document from beginning to end. It was written in a time when Christians faced increasing pressure to synchronize their lives according to the political visions of the Roman Empire, up to and including worship of the emperor as a god. New Testament scholar Craig Koester helps bring the mystery of Revelation into focus in demonstrating that Revelation "gives alternating messages of warning and encouragement that are designed to promote faithful endurance" in the face of mounting pressure to concede to the Roman Empire's practices of cult worship.[25] As Revelation was written, "to refuse to accord divine honors to Domitian [the Roman emperor] could be considered an act of political disloyalty or even treason."[26] In a time of rapid societal and political changes, "The church was in a transitional and vulnerable situation," Eugene Boring writes, "trying to find its way forward in the generation between the death of its apostolic leaders and the emergence of a firm structure and sense of self-identity. What did it mean to be Christian, to try to follow Jesus as Lord, in such a place and time?"[27]

The questions of what kind of political vision the church will adopt have everything to do with how they truly understand the reality of their faith to be lived out. Either Jesus is Lord or Caesar is; Christians will need to decide which political vision they will follow.

---

25. Craig R. Koester, *Revelation and the End of All Things* (Grand Rapids: Wm. B. Eerdmans Publishing Co., 2001), 30.

26. M. Eugene Boring, *Revelation* (Louisville: John Knox Press, 1989), 21.

27. Ibid.

The choices facing Christians in the time of John's revelation are not unlike the choices facing Christians today, in terms of the vision that will guide our engagement in the political world. While it would be an overstatement to say that Christians living in North America at the dawn of the twenty-first century are enduring the same pressing concerns as Christians living in first-century Rome, we can see that the choice between political visions essentially progresses along two general lines: the world of kings or the world of the kingdom.

Each of those worlds understands politics to serve a different goal, or end. For some, the end of politics is that they amass power. Others may see that, on its better days, the end of politics is to establish justice. In the late modern world, justice is often understood as the establishment of a condition in which the rights of certain persons are not transgressed by other persons. Especially in a Western political vision, such as in the United States, justice looks a lot like citizens giving one another enough space that no one's rights are infringed upon: Everyone gets to do what they want to do freely, without someone else restricting that freedom. In many contemporary legal battles, the question of whose rights have been violated is the most pressing issue being debated.

At the end of the day, the great hope of Western democracy is this: *We all need to give one another space to pursue our own ends without unnecessary interference from anyone else.* "Life, liberty, and the pursuit of happiness" require that we uphold and respect one another's autonomy and freedom so that everyone is truly free to pursue whatever happiness may look like for each individual. According to this vision, the model society is comprised of a collection of individuals who really don't need to have much to do with one another, so long as they respect one another's space and don't violate the others' rights.

To be sure, this vision of the end of politics has deeply shaped us, and it has deeply shaped the church, particularly in North America. The end of politics given to us in Revelation, however, is different, and this is a rather uncomfortable reality with which Western democratic Christians have wrestled academically, but rarely societally. Whereas the end of politics for Western democracy is tolerance, the end of politics in Revelation is reconciliation. While the world of kings may be able to deliver tolerance in some form or fashion, it is only the world of the kingdom that can ultimately take us to reconciliation.

Look, for example, at the way Revelation concludes, particularly with the vision of the New Jerusalem, the crowning glory of the new creation that God has brought into reality. In the initial unveiling of the great city, John hears a political declaration about the way life will be ordered within its walls: "God's dwelling place is now among the people, and he will dwell with them. They will be his people, and God himself will be with them and be their God" (Revelation 21:3). The measurements of the city are also beautifully fascinating, quantified in units of twelve, with a gate assigned to each of the twelve tribes of Israel (Revelation 21:12), signifying a fulfillment of Israel, while also measuring higher, wider, and longer than the known universe of John's day. Additionally, the gates of the city are now open, raising the question, *If this city is larger than the known world, who is left to enter the gates?* This is the kind of question that probably isn't meant to have a simple answer; the question itself tells us more than the answer. The fulfillment of creation will be marked with God's dwelling with the people, it will be a fulfillment of what God has always intended for humanity, and it will forever stand open to those who wish to take up residence in that city according to the new political order of God's reconciliation.

"The nations will walk by its light," we are told in 21:24, and "the glory and honor of the nations will be brought into it" in 21:26, all of which has something to do with the fruit-bearing trees that line the river flowing through the city, the leaves of which "are for the healing of the nations" in 22:2. In this short collection of verses, something becomes strikingly clear about what God is doing politically: The characteristic and violent mark of international relationships throughout Scripture has been erased, and the nations now live according to the reconciliation of God's peace. We should also notice that the nations do not need to be dominated by one empire to establish peace, nor are the distinguishing characteristics of each nation erased. What is now different is that they walk according to the rhythms and logic of the kingdom, rather than the rhythms and logic of their kings.

In the same way that Genesis 1 and 2 tell us something about what it means to be human in relationship to a creator God, Revelation 21 and 22 tell us something about what it means to be political creatures in God's creation. In the garden, humans and God lived in conciliation. The *shalom* of life in the garden came as the humans lived in God's presence, and that same *shalom* is reestablished as humans once again live in God's presence in the new creation. As God reconciles creation to God's own self, humans are also made to live in reconciliation with one another.

Notice that the nations do not merely tolerate one another; rather, they live in reconciled peace with one another. While tolerance is given as a secondary gift to creation as we await the new creation, we cannot come to a place where we assume that tolerance is the true end of politics. As those who await God's new creation, we do so with a sanctified vision of politics, seeing that political life and ordering has always been most truly about being reconciled to God and, thus, to one another, walking in the *shalom* of God's presence, rather than simply giving one another enough space that we do not violate one another's rights. Tolerance is not a bad thing, but we need to acknowledge that a Christian view of politics, a sanctified vision of what politics is meant for, is so much more than simply putting up with one another. Instead, it is intended to be the language we speak when it comes to living now, according to the full reality of what is yet to come.

When theologians speak about this kind of thing, they often describe it as "eschatological," meaning that it has everything to do with

God's future breaking into our present. What might it mean for God's vision of the end of politics to break into our present? In what we have seen from God's salvation history, political association was never *for* tolerance. We thank God that God has seen fit to give us rulers to establish tolerance in this period before the new creation, but at its fullest and deepest, politics has always been about being reconciled to God and to one another. How, then, might that begin to challenge the ways in which we live now? How might we live in such a way that we are making way for God's future to break into our present?

We would be remiss if we left these ideas to be interpreted in such a way to think that, somehow, we can begin the work of reconciliation on our own, making a way for God's kingdom to come by our political efforts. Indeed, Paul's instructions on reconciliation leave no room for such an interpretation. Rather, he draws together the themes of new creation and reconciliation in a way that tells us that a life of reconciliation comes as a gift of God, and that gift's name was Jesus of Nazareth. "All this is from God," Paul writes, "who reconciled us to himself through Christ and gave us the ministry of reconciliation: that God was reconciling the world to himself in Christ..." (2 Corinthians 5:18-19). By virtue of what God has done, Paul reminds us, we have the opportunity to be reconciled now, among the political visions of tolerance and among the logic and rhythms of the kingdoms of this world, which may be able to establish tolerance, but never reconciliation. The eschatological and sanctified vision of political life for Christians is that, by virtue of what God has done to reconcile us to God, we can also live in reconciliation with one another, taking our cues from the reality of God's future and living it out by God's grace in our present.

So what is politics for? What is its end? It is ultimately to live in reconciliation, a reality that comes only as we live in reconciliation to God. Until all of creation comes to that point and the New Jerusalem is presently in view, we are grateful for the places where tolerance takes the place of injustice, acknowledging that there are times in which we are called to act against injustice on tolerance's behalf. But for the Christian, for the one who has a sanctified vision of political life, we recognize that we do not live for tolerance, but for reconciliation. And in view of the bold absurdity of God becoming human, we also see that God's future has already broken into our present and that, by virtue of God reconciling us to God's self in Christ, we are given every permission to live in reconciliation with one another—not to merely tolerate the other but to live now according to the logic and rhythms of the kingdom that is still coming in its fullness.

So what are the specific ways in which we live this out? To be sure, it will look different from place to place and situation to situation. It will also take Christians discerning together the ways in which we might most faithfully live God's political future in the midst of the present, a task that will require lots of conversation and truth-seeking. It will, most certainly, require that Christians come to be able to see that the logic and rhythms of the world of kings is often highly effective at establishing tolerance, but Christians should not be satisfied with mere tolerance; rather, they should develop an eschatological craving for the rhythms and logic of the kingdom and a longing for a sanctified vision of political life.

But if there is any pastoral advice we might give on where to begin to establish a sanctified vision of political life, it would be to hear Paul's own admonition: "We implore you on Christ's behalf: Be reconciled to God" (2 Corinthians 5:20). May we, having glimpsed the political goodness of God's new creation, have our political vision sanctified by God's grace, that we might see that politics is neither for the amassment of power to the benefit of a few, nor is it even ultimately to establish tolerance. May we see that politics, according to the rhythms and logic of the kingdom, is for reconciliation, the lasting *shalom* that comes as God's gift to a creation that longs to be made new.

THE RECOUNT

The World of Kings:	The World of the Kingdom:
Sees the world in terms of competing powers	Sees the world in terms of God's faithfulness to sustain the meek and humble
Trusts in a certain kind of news source and has trouble hearing good news from untrusted sources	Is willing to receive good news from those who may be considered outsiders
Uses politics to promote the leaders' agendas	Uses politics to establish reconciliation among and between people
Can tolerate others	Can be reconciled to others

AFTERWORD

In the introduction, we said that our hope was to draw you into the world of 2 Kings and to let it begin to shape the way you see political life. That kind of approach to a book about politics doesn't exactly lend itself to a clear-cut set of instructions on what one ought to do politically, how one should vote, or what party one ought to support. As we conclude, we hope you've come to realize that, rather than giving short answers to complex questions, our purpose was to draw you into the narrative of 2 Kings and let Scripture form a different political vision of the world for you.

That political vision is native to the book of 2 Kings, but it's also influenced by what we see in the life and ministry of Jesus, and we couldn't wrap up this book without making that influence overt. Philippians 2:6-8 gives us an arrestingly beautiful image of Jesus:

Who, being in very nature God,
> did not consider equality with God something to be used to
> > his own advantage;
rather, he made himself nothing
> by taking the very nature of a servant,
> being made in human likeness.
And being found in appearance as a man,
> he humbled himself
> by becoming obedient to death—
> > even death on a cross!

The day Paul penned those words in his letter to the Philippians, the political message would have been unmistakable. The symbol of the cross was a symbol of Rome's political power and authority, and anyone who heard Paul's letter would understand the implications. But there is a powerful political reversal in Philippians 2. By invoking the cross, Paul points us toward the political world of kings and silently asks us to consider the means and methods of that political world.

Rome's political power was born out of a cycle of threat, fear, punishment, violence, and crucifixion. Rome's political rulers became powerful precisely because they could appeal to the cross in a very public way. The more Roman citizens who witnessed a public crucifixion, the more reluctant Roman citizens would become to challenge the authority of the rulers, which gave the rulers more power. Roman rulers became more powerful as they sought to build themselves up by crucifying their enemies. The cycle seemed endless.

But the cross played a different role in the world of the kingdom. Jesus reversed the cycle. His approach to the cross was one of self-emptying, rather than self-promotion. Rather than ascent to political power, his movement is one of descent toward humility. And somehow, this is the way God works. This great reversal is the rhythm of life in the world of the kingdom. It is the alternative logic that counteracts the world of kings, subverting and overcoming violence, fear, and punishment at the very moment it encounters an ascent to power and responds in humility. Nothing about the way of Jesus Christ makes sense to the world of kings. And yet this is the way God has chosen to redeem the world.

We realize that the world of the kingdom may not be as well equipped at "getting things done" in the world of kings. But we're also pretty sure that getting things done isn't what the world of the kingdom is about, at least in terms of what that means in the world of kings. Engaging the world of politics from a perspective of the world of the kingdom will require a grace-filled persistence that holds faithfulness in higher regard than effectiveness. But the faithful engagement by a grace-transformed people just may be the way God has been getting things done for generations.

Of course, persistence is not always passive, but in the world of the kingdom, it is always directed at peace and reconciliation. And the times in which we are called to persistently engage will require a Spirit-led process of discernment. If you're wondering, *So what exactly are we supposed to do politically?* our guidance would be something along the lines of: Gather with other believers, empty yourself, lovingly deliberate, humbly discern, and then go and be persistent. Engage the world according to the way of Jesus Christ in the power of the Holy Spirit. Take the vision that the ancient stories of our faith open to us and act according to the world of the kingdom.

This doesn't always mean we will begin at a place of agreement with one another on how we ought to engage a particular political issue, but it does mean a common goal will be required of us, and that goal is shown to us in the world of the kingdom. It is God's peace, justice, and deep reconciliation. Engaging with the world of the kingdom in view will mean we may need to lay down some of our previously held political convictions if those convictions have been formed in us by a story that is not our own. Holding tightly to political convictions is no virtue if those convictions are not aimed at kingdom purposes. The world of the kingdom asks us to incorporate previously unheard voices in our processes of deliberation and discernment, and to consider the way the voices of the powerless can often deliver news of salvation if we would but hear them speak.

Perhaps, then, there is something of the holy in the practice of politics according to the world of the kingdom. It may just be that, so long as our guiding vision of political engagement is aimed at God's purposes of justice, peace, and reconciliation, political life could have everything to do with holiness. But we must also have the humility and courage to step into a story larger than ourselves and allow that story to teach us what those purposes might actually be, rather than pursuing our own agendas with religious fervor.

For this reason, we are moved to gratitude that God has not released us to our own devices when it comes to political life. God has given us a story of the Father, Son, and Holy Spirit, a story that has a way of making our own agendas look small when we are willing to admit it, but grace enough to bring us to that point. May our engagement reflect the holiness of a God who is working in the life of that people called the church, a people whose story is being written according to the rhythms and patterns of the world of the kingdom of God.